PRICE GUIDE (usually refers to

£   inexpensive – up to about

££   moderate   – up to about £20 for two courses

£££ expensive   – over £20 for two courses

These are estimates only, based on the approximate cost of an à la carte meal for one.

THE GLASGOW 100

THE INDEPENDENT GUIDE TO
THE BEST PLACES TO EAT

David Phillips

Luath Press Limited

EDINBURGH

www.luath.co.uk

First Published as Eating Out in Glasgow by Richard Drew Publishing
4th Edition 2004

The paper used in this book is acid-free and recyclable. It is made
from low chlorine pulps produced in a low energy, low emission
manner from sustainable forests.

Printed and bound by
Nørhaven Paperback A/S, Denmark

Typeset in Meta by S. Fairgrieve, Edinburgh 0131 658 1763

Dedication
To Zelda and Fred

CONTENTS

INTRODUCTION

Glasgow's recent cultural and commercial renaissance has been well documented. The service sector, including catering, now employs more people on Clydeside than the shipyards did in their heyday. The visual evidence is unmistakable. The visitor or resident is confronted with a plethora of smart cafés, bistros, gastropubs and restaurants of every conceivable style. This is excellent news.

The bad news is that quality is far from consistent. Compared to most other British cities, Glaswegians may be fortunate though mediocrity remains rife. And at the top end of the market, the picture is far from rosy. Since the sad demise of Gordon Ramsay's *Amaryllis*, Glasgow has had nothing remotely comparable to, say, London's *Savoy Grill, L'Escargot* or *The Capital*. Top flight cooking, waitering and managerial skills are just too thin on the ground north of the border.

Even if you just want a decent rather than a superlative meal, choosing a restaurant at random from the enormous selection on offer is a risky business. Do you really want to play a gastronomic lottery in which the unpredictable outcome ranges from total satisfaction to a severe gastro-intestinal upset or worse – not to mention the irreversible damage you might inflict on your wallet? We all recognise the Scots' penchant for sugar, fizzy drinks and saturated fat and most of us try to keep these under control. But there are numerous other hazards including absurdly loud 'background' music, rickety furniture and – most lethal of all – second-hand cigarette smoke, although the Scottish Parliament has announced plans to introduce a ban on smoking in public places from 2006.

So much for the future – what about the present? Fortunately, you can have an extremely enjoyable meal in Glasgow but you have to know where to find it. If you are unfamiliar with the city and are looking for a recommended place to eat, this is the book for you. And even if you are Glaswegian born and bred, and have your own personal favourite eating places, this guide is equally desirable as you cannot possibly keep up to date with the rapid changes that are taking place in the city's culinary scene.

Let me state at the outset that this selection of 100 eating places is a highly personal one. Nevertheless, the assessment criteria I have applied will, I believe, secure widespread support from discerning diners. These are: food quality, efficiency and friendliness of service, general ambience and value for money. The ideal eating place will score highly in all four dimensions. That doesn't mean that all the restaurants appearing in the guide have attained absolute perfection. Far from it – many of the reviews contain constructive criticisms where one or more of the criteria leave something to be desired. But every entry is a recommendation, nevertheless, and I recognise that readers' views may differ sharply from mine in some cases. That's fine by me. The ability to agree to disagree is the hallmark of a civilised society.

All of the reviews were conducted anonymously, and I accepted no 'hospitality' from the listed establishments. The guide has been produced without the support of sponsors or advertisers. Readers may therefore be assured that the judgements I have made are totally independent of any pecuniary incentives, commercial pressures or subtle cajoling of any kind.

Bon appetit!

David Phillips

WEST END

The West End is usually regarded as the most attractive part of Central Glasgow. Dominated by the impressive Gilbert Scott Building of Glasgow University, Kelvingrove Park forms a delightfully lush centrepiece to the area. The main thoroughfare is Byres Road (Hillhead subway station) which runs from stately Great Western Road at the top (north) end down to bustling Partick Cross at the bottom. Apart from the University, with its fine Hunterian Museum and Gallery, other highlights include the Museum of Transport and the Kelvingrove Museum (currently undergoing refurbishment). Further to the north and west are the prosperous suburbs of Bearsden and Milngavie (pronounced Mull-Guy).

AIR ORGANIC

36 Kelvingrove Street   0141 564 5200

The precise derivation of the name is obscure but you'll encounter organic produce served in a futuristic space with airline connotations. If that doesn't sound enthralling, focus on the food. You can eat snacks in the downstairs bar, with an extension into an open-air south facing trench-like patio at the front, or you climb the steps (via a different entrance) into the main restaurant. Here, a cheery server hands you an airline ticket (the menu) that lists an

Sunday brunch receives rave reviews.

interesting mix of offerings spanning vegetarian, meat and fish dishes. They do strange and delightful things to simple pastas, pizzas and burgers and nothing is quite what it seems. Vaguely oriental ingredients such as chives, lemon, mango and cashew nuts are deployed with great flair. Starters and salads are particularly innovative. Sunday brunch receives rave reviews. The management are obviously looking skywards and prices are following suit so you might do well to have the set lunch (about £10).

FOOD STYLE **INTERNATIONAL**
LICENSED **YES**
NON-SMOKING TABLES **YES**
WHEELCHAIR ACCESS **NO**
OPEN **SUN–THUR NOON-10PM**
      FRI–SAT NOON-10.30PM
PRICE **££**

ARCAFFE

11 North Claremont Street   0141 333 1333

This is the quintessential café that is much more than a café. Regarded as a lunchtime oasis for harassed local office and clinic workers, who would defend it with their lives, Arcaffe is tucked into a quiet street off a part of Sauchiehall Street that few visitors encounter. There's a delightful Eastern Mediterranean atmosphere here from the picturesque décor (including an imposing geographical mural) to the bowl of olives awaiting you on the table. Because the welcoming staff are mainly permanent rather than casual workers, they exhibit a rare degree of polish and expertise that is somehow deeply reassuring. The (largely Italian) menu caters for most tastes and appetites. Pizzas and pastas are, of course, excellent, as are starters, salads

Go out of your way to sample the beautifully prepared smoked salmon

and desserts. Go out of your way to sample the beautifully prepared smoked salmon and any of the pastas with an unrivalled arabiata sauce. Portions are ample and the prices acceptable if not exactly rock bottom. Coffee comes in a range of speciality formats.

FOOD STYLE **ITALIAN/MEDITERRANEAN**
LICENSED **YES**
NON-SMOKING TABLES **YES**
WHEELCHAIR ACCESS **YES**
OPEN **MON–FRI 9AM-3PM**
PRICE **£**

The ASHOKA
108 Elderslie Street   0141 221 1761

Unrelated to its namesakes around the city, the Ashoka was a pioneer of the Glasgow Indian restaurant scene in the 1970s. An impressive array of awards, certificates and letters of appreciation adorn the walls. On two levels (the upper floor threatening karaoke), the rooms are spacious, elegant and comfortable with slightly decadent red décor much in evidence. The efficient staff are courteous without being obsequious. In summer, you might brave the elements and eat in the delightful little garden below street level. The menu has some distinctly exotic features – Kashmiri pakora comprises banana, pineapple and other fruits fried in batter. The Parsi dishes, believed to originate from Persia, are exquisite with numerous unusual vegetables cooked in olive oil with subtly flavoured herbs and spices. Side dishes – especially pashwari naans – are enjoyable. Not cheap but lunch and pre-theatre deals are outstanding. The wine list is surprisingly extensive. The only jarring feature is the inexplicably occidental background music.

Lunch and pre-theatre deals are outstanding

FOOD STYLE **INDIAN**
LICENSED **YES**
NON-SMOKING TABLES **NO**
WHEELCHAIR ACCESS **NO**
OPEN **MON–SAT 11AM-MIDNIGHT**
     SUN NOON-MIDNIGHT
PRICE **££**

ASHOKA ASHTON LANE

19 Ashton Lane   0141 337 1115 or 0800 195 3195

Arguably the jewel in the Harlequin chain, this Ashoka has benefited hugely from the inspired managerial decision to ban smoking. At last, you can inhale the pungent aromas of the Punjab without risking a heart attack or lung cancer. The room is not especially spacious so you are safer booking ahead – especially if you fancy one of the more secluded booths that line the walls. The menu is a little more restricted than many Indian restau-

The house specialities are quite simply brilliant

rants but that's probably a strength. Haggis pakora may catch your eye but the vegetable version is one of the finest in Scotland. The house specialities are quite simply brilliant – especially Jalfrezi or Pardesi with chicken or lamb. There's a tempting list of tandoori dishes and plenty of vegetarian choices. Wash down the generous portions with excellent Indian beer. The two course lunch (£6.95) and pre-theatre (£8.95) deals offer unrivalled value, and children (accompanied by an adult) eat free on Sunday.

Highly recommended

FOOD STYLE **INDIAN**
LICENSED **YES**
NON-SMOKING TABLES **YES**
WHEELCHAIR ACCESS **NO**
OPEN **MON–THUR NOON-MIDNIGHT**
      FRI–SAT NOON-12.30AM
      SUN 5PM-MIDNIGHT
PRICE **££**

ASIA STYLE

185 St Georges Road   0141 332 8828

The St Georges Cross district has long lacked a proper restaurant and now it has one. Mind you, the name must be ironic, at least as far as the décor is concerned. Fortunately, it seems spotlessly clean and you gaze directly into the open kitchen. You are handed a menu that, with luck, is in English, on which you mark your choices. If this bemuses you, as it probably will, check out the specials and then converse with the affable staff. You are in the world of Malaysian Chinese food with few concessions made to western tastes. Tempted as you might be by a thousand year-old egg, or a rice-based dish called porridge, I suggest you leave those to the Malaysian regulars and opt for duck, seafood, fish or beef dishes. Vegetarians beware – the chef has a habit of throwing some diced pork into the mix when you least expect it. Portions are substantial and the prices modest. Copious quantities of tea keeps your palate fresh.

The St Georges Cross district has long lacked a proper restaurant and now it has one

FOOD STYLE **CHINESE/MALAYSIAN**
LICENSED **YES**
NON-SMOKING TABLES **NO**
WHEELCHAIR ACCESS **YES**
OPEN **SUN–SAT 5PM-3AM**
PRICE **££**

BAR MILANO
4/10 Byres Road   0141 357 3063

The Partick Cross end of Byres Road was once considered distinctly infra-dig but no longer. There is a cluster of top-notch eateries down here and Bar Milano regards itself, with some justification, as one of them. The opening of a second branch at Eastwood Toll on the South Side may have stretched the managerial capacity a little. Nevertheless, you'll usually get a warm (and, if you're lucky, eye-catching) welcome to this bright and spacious restaurant that has sensibly banished smokers to the upper section. The staff are skilled, friendly and happy to offer opinions. The menu is less predictable than you might expect with numerous seafood and vegetarian options. Meat-eaters are positively pandered to here – the varieties of veal are especially tempting. Of the pastas, spinach and ricotta ravioli is hard to beat. Portion sizes are variable but mostly generous. Predictably, decent quality ice cream adorns several creditable desserts. Lunch, pre-theatre and other deals represent excellent value.

Welcome to this bright and spacious restaurant

FOOD STYLE **ITALIAN**
LICENSED **YES**
NON-SMOKING TABLES **YES**
WHEELCHAIR ACCESS **YES**
OPEN **MON–SUN NOON-11PM**
PRICE **££**

The BAY TREE CAFÉ
403 Great Western Road   0141 334 5898

The bad news first – this once vegan restaurant now serves meat. What's the point of being semi-vegetarian, even if the meat is cooked separately? The good news is that the food is excellent. Now mainly Middle Eastern, you can indulge in lashings of hummus, pitta, felafel, rice (saffron no less) and couscous. Blackboard specials are worth a detour – Arabian aubergine bake is magnificent – and the staff will opine on the best bet. Salads are fresh, exotic and colourful. Portions are generous and the service friendly. Desserts include wonderful baklava and Turkish Delight but watch out for the potent coffee – this stuff will give you insomnia for a week. The décor is somewhat basic though the potted plants and quirky paintings enliven the scene. There are outside tables should the sun ever shine on this side of the street. Unlicensed but you can BYOB. Remarkable value, even without the ten percent student discount.

Blackboard specials are worth a detour – Arabian aubergine bake is magnificent

Highly recommended

FOOD STYLE **MIDDLE EASTERN**
LICENSED **No**
NON-SMOKING TABLES **No**
WHEELCHAIR ACCESS **YES**
OPEN **MON–SAT 9.30AM-10PM**
          SUN 9.30AM-9PM
PRICE **£**

BREL

39 Ashton Lane   0141 342 4966

There are several fine restaurants in Ashton Lane and Brel is one of the best. Once a stable, the atmosphere is unique – eccentric, youthful and noisy, especially when the jazz or folk bands are belting it out in the rear lounge. Turn a blind eye to the unprepossessing entrance, the sombre décor, the strange tablecloths. Just take a deep breath and you'll be fine. Especially when you've tasted the excellent food – moules-frites is the obvious choice but who could resist

Repeat this mantra to yourself – mustn't miss the mousse

wild boar sausage and apple with leek mash or diced lamb with feta, red wine and tarragon? If those sound odd, what about a Brel Atkins platter of cold meats, olives and salad? You're encouraged to wash that lot down with Belgian draught beer (an acquired taste) or at least with a bottle of perfectly decent and inexpensive house wine. Towards the end of the meal, repeat this mantra to yourself – mustn't miss the mousse. Good value, particularly early evening.

FOOD STYLE **BELGIAN**
LICENSED **YES**
NON-SMOKING TABLES **NO**
WHEELCHAIR ACCESS **YES**
OPEN **MON– FRI NOON-3PM 5-10.30PM**
         SAT– SUN NOON-10.30PM
PRICE **££**

The CABIN
996 Dumbarton Road   0141 569 1036

I defy you to find anything quite like this anywhere else in Europe. The Cabin is located in a deeply unfashionable part of the West End so there's virtually no passing trade. Denis Dwyer, the chef-proprietor, has found a successful formula and has stuck to it for more than a decade. The setting can't be the attraction – the dining area is hardly opulent and the furniture is, shall we say, eccentric. By contrast, everything on the menu is eye-catching. Scottish

I defy you to find anything quite like this anywhere else in Europe

ingredients (beef, venison, fish) are combined with Irish cooking to produce a kind of Celtic crossover style. This may be unorthodox but the resultant meals are remarkably satisfying, from the home-made soup all the way to the accomplished dessert.

Though open for lunch and pre-theatre, there's only one sitting for dinner, an experience that turns out to be theatrical in more than one sense. For reasons beyond the comprehension of this writer, regulars never seem to tire of the communal sing-song led, invariably at full throttle, by the irrepressible Wilma.

FOOD STYLE **SCOTTISH/IRISH**
LICENSED **YES**
NON-SMOKING TABLES **No**
WHEELCHAIR ACCESS **No**
OPEN **TUE–FRI NOON-2PM**
    5.30-6.45 PM (PRE-THEATRE)
    7.30 FOR 8PM (ONE SITTING ONLY)
    SAT 7.30 FOR 8PM (ONE SITTING ONLY)
    CLOSED SUN–MON
PRICE **£££**

CAFÉ ANDALUZ

2 Cresswell Lane   0141 339 1111

When the old Underground Café closed several years ago, local anxiety about its replacement was almost palpable. Fortunately, a more than worthy successor occupies the site. The transformation of the entire cellar from a staid Scots tearoom into a lively Spanish restaurant is brilliant. The strikingly coloured wall tiles, the elaborately carved furniture and the clever lighting all combine to create a truly Mediterranean ambience. The place

Regularly full and buzzing with a hundred conversations

is regularly full and buzzing with a hundred conversations aided by excellent Rioja. The menu is fairly simple with clear instructions about how to order tapas. There are over 30 on offer of which about half are vegetarian, the rest divided between meat, seafood and fish.

Alternatively there are a few paellas (including one made only from rice and vegetables) and specials. Each tapas dish is about £3-4. Wise choices include tortilla (Spanish omelette), esparragos con huevas (fresh asparagus with grated egg), pinchito de pollo (skewers of lemon and mint flavoured chicken) and carne de res (thinly sliced beef). Over-stretched staff (mostly) retain a pleasant demeanour.

FOOD STYLE **SPANISH**
LICENSED **YES**
NON-SMOKING TABLES **YES**
WHEELCHAIR ACCESS **NO**
OPEN **MON–SAT NOON-11PM**
       SUN 12.30PM-10.30PM
PRICE **££**

CAFÉ ANTIPASTI
337 Byres Road   0141 337 2737

Of the two branches, this one has the edge on its
Sauchiehall Street twin (0141 332 9002). Much more than
a café, Antipasti seems permanently packed, partly no
doubt to the limited space. The big glass frontage suggests a zero tolerance of privacy but the mezzanine floor
is less accessible to the gaze of curious passers-by. More
alluring features include the chunky wooden tables,
stylish crockery and a broad pavement for summer
tables. The menu has all the predictable sections – pasta, pizza, fish,
chicken – but look a little closer and
you'll discover highly imaginative
combinations of fresh local produce
with less familiar vegetables, fruits,
herbs and spices. Ever tried extra
virgin rubbed swordfish, chargrilled with focaccia croutons? Or braised lamb, on the shank, slow cooked with
potatoes, carrots, shallots and celery, drenched with its
slow cooked juices? Didn't think so. The tasty baking and
quality coffee make an ideal partnership if you're not in
the market for a full meal.

The tasty baking and quality coffee make an ideal partnership

FOOD STYLE **ITALIAN**
LICENSED **YES**
NON-SMOKING TABLES **YES**
WHEELCHAIR ACCESS **YES**
OPEN **MON–SUN NOON-MIDNIGHT**
PRICE **££**

CAFÉ JJ
180 Dumbarton Road   0141 357 1881

This part of Dumbarton Road is changing rapidly but not this gem of a café, too easily overlooked, near Partick Cross. The initial impression is deceptive – the room is larger than you think though it gets choc-a-bloc – with good reason – at lunchtime. Decorated in warm, inviting colours, the atmosphere is welcoming and comfortable. The menu runs the gamut from toasties, baked potatoes and burgers to more ambitious crêpes, sausages and the famous peat-smoked haddock. Watch out for changing blackboard specials about which the staff will offer sound advice. Especially memorable are fresh vegetable soups and any of the superb home made desserts. Coffee is good but the tea is even better. Portions are sizeable without being unmanageable. The small wine list has been thoughtfully composed. Prices are fair and there are early evening special deals. Opening hours are somewhat eccentric. This is one you'll want to revisit again and again.

Especially memorable are fresh vegetable soups and any of the superb home made desserts

FOOD STYLE **INTERNATIONAL**
LICENSED **YES**
NON-SMOKING TABLES **YES**
WHEELCHAIR ACCESS **YES**
OPEN **MON–WED 11AM-7.30PM**
      THUR–SAT 11AM-10.30PM
      SUN NOON-6PM
PRICE **£**

CITY CAFÉ
Finnieston Quay   0141 227 1010

This misleadingly named hotel restaurant occupies an enviable spot on the riverside close to some of Glasgow's most curious artefacts (North Rotunda, Finnieston Crane). The south-facing dining area is permanently bathed in light. In summer you might sit on the terrace or simply gaze out of the wide glass window. The bar menu looks modest enough with its disappointingly narrow range of soups, salads, sandwiches and burgers but that may give the wrong impression as you get fresh, high quality food presented more than competently. If you are looking for something more sophisticated, the showcase Kitchen Menu is preferable, from which you might choose pigeon for starter, roast cod for main and end with iced coconut parfait. The chef clearly selects his ingredients carefully and is particularly adept with anything from the sea. Sauces and dressings often have a pleasing oriental take and the side dishes are delectable. None of this comes cheap – wine by the glass offering especially dubious value.

> *The south-facing dining area is permanently bathed in light*

FOOD STYLE **SCOTTISH/INTERNATIONAL**
LICENSED **YES**
NON-SMOKING TABLES **YES**
WHEELCHAIR ACCESS **YES**
OPEN **MON–SAT 6.45-9.30AM NOON-2.30PM 6-10.30PM**
SUN 7-9.30AM NOON-2.30PM 6-9.30PM
PRICE **££**

The COOK'S ROOM
13 Woodside Crescent   0141 353 0707

Owner Tom Battersby was absolutely right to relocate from cramped premises in Giffnock to the more spacious basement vacated by Nick Nairn. While not quite in the celebrity chef league, Battersby is winning an ever-widening circle of admirers who are beating a path to his door in Charing Cross. The room has lost the sometimes stifling formality imposed by its previous occupier and is none the worse for that

This is serious cooking displaying a high degree of skill

although the mix of furniture styles looks odd. The menu is mainstream Scottish with French and oriental touches, a generally successful combination that obviously appeals to Glaswegian palates. Epithets such as 'homely' or 'rustic' have been applied but could mislead. This is serious cooking displaying a high degree of skill that effectively combines local produce with exquisite sauces and dressings. Venison and poultry dishes are among the most memorable, though fish lovers won't see past a superbly judged halibut steak. Changing desserts are worth a second glance – almond or pear tart should not be resisted.

FOOD STYLE **SCOTTISH**

LICENSED **YES**

NON-SMOKING TABLES **YES**

WHEELCHAIR ACCESS **NO**

OPEN **MON–SAT NOON-2.30PM 5.30-9.30PM**
        CLOSED SUN

PRICE **££(£)**

COTTIERS
93-95 Hyndland Street   0141 357 5825

Churches that are converted to restaurants exert a peculiar fascination for Scots – perhaps they epitomise the secular age. In the case of Cottiers, the transformation of the former Dowanhill Parish Church is triumphant. The complex boasts a cavernous but atmospheric bar where you can buy snacks, an appealing beer garden when weather permits, a 350-seat theatre and a loft restaurant at the top of a steep staircase. The décor is a little crude but somehow that matters little. The menu skirts around the Gulf of Mexico and offers a formidable range of dishes from basic tortillas and burgers to fajitas and enchiladas. Diners preferring something more British can opt for lamb cooked with lime or brisket of beef. Vegetarians aren't neglected either. Look out for the 30% discount in the early evening on some dishes. Service is mostly efficient and welcoming. The noise level can be massive during the office party season.

The menu skirts around the Gulf of Mexico and offers a formidable range of dishes

FOOD STYLE **AMERICAN/INTERNATIONAL**
LICENSED **YES**
NON-SMOKING TABLES **NO**
WHEELCHAIR ACCESS **NO**
OPEN **MON–FRI 5-10.30PM**
    SAT 5-11PM
    SUN NOON-10.30PM
PRICE **££**

DI MAGGIOS

18 Gibson Street   0141 357 3063

Don't underestimate Di Maggios. While pandering unashamedly to the mainstream pizza and pasta market, they do this with great aplomb and have been rewarded by a large following across the West of Scotland. The Gibson Street branch, in the heart of studentland, is one of two in the West End, the other being in nearby Ruthven Lane (0141 334 6000) off Byres Road. The room is smallish, enhanced by a cleverly placed long mirror on one wall, and has an appealingly intimate mezzanine floor. As well as the standard and highly reliable Italian fare, the weekend brunch (comprising such delicacies as french toast and omelettes) is worth seeking out. The red house wine generally has the edge over the white. Coffee is respectable, served with a wafer, though no refills were offered. Staff are good-natured and child-friendly. Prices are reasonable. You are unlikely to be overwhelmed by the Di Maggios experience but you should be cheered by it all the same.

*Don't underestima
Di Maggios*

FOOD STYLE **ITALIAN**
LICENSED **YES**
NON-SMOKING TABLES **NO**
WHEELCHAIR ACCESS **YES**
OPEN **SUN–THUR NOON-11PM**
         FRI–SAT NOON-MIDNIGHT
PRICE **££**

The DINING ROOM
41 Byres Road   0141 339 3666

Once you've got over the shock of the sheer compactness of the place, you can start to enjoy truly accomplished cooking. Co-owner Jim Kerr has established a deserved reputation for leading the pack of a new generation of chefs who create wonderful linkages between local produce and global cuisine. Looking eastwards towards Japan as much as Thailand, Kerr has constructed a menu of commendable flair. A remarkable sashimi combination of thinly sliced halibut, scallop and bream dressed with olive oil, lemon, ginger and chives may be too challenging a starter for some, in which case go for the delicately spiced vegetable and herb soup. Conventional meat dishes such as roast lamb or beef are brilliantly improved by inventive garnishing imbued with basil, cumin and other intriguingly elusive flavours. Fish, seafood and poultry are all handled with supreme confidence, as are desserts. Not cheap, of course, except for the bargain price set lunch (about £11). Watch out for smokers on the mezzanine floor.

Fish, seafood and poultry are all handled with supreme confidence

Highly recommended

FOOD STYLE **SCOTTISH**
LICENSED **YES**
NON-SMOKING TABLES **YES**
WHEELCHAIR ACCESS **NO**
OPEN **TUE–WED, SAT–SUN 5.30-11PM; THUR–FRI NOON-2.30PM, 5.30-11PM. CLOSED MON**
PRICE **£££**

EDEN
168 Hyndland Road   0141 339 0111

Hyndland is Glasgow's Hampstead, full of leafy lanes, sophisticated shops, charming delis – though sadly unblessed by NW3's profusion of good cafés and restaurants. Eden goes some way towards rectifying that.

Passers-by may think it's just a hairdressing salon but the lower floor houses a beauty shop and a bistro. At first glance you might think this is an unremarkable café but you'd be wrong. The menu has all the usual snacks (baked potatoes, sandwiches, salads) but you can also order tapas, nachos and paellas. A long list of blackboard specials, constantly being updated, gives the game away. Someone around here is deeply committed to quality food. If you're sceptical, order fresh, richly flavoured home-made tomato soup with croutons and parsley (served with fresh chunks of brown bread) followed by nicely garnished smoked haddock or poached salmon and you'll be converted. For under a tenner, you can wash that lot down with a bottle of house wine and sober up with the punchy black coffee. Terrific concept, brilliantly executed.

Someone around here is deeply committed to quality food

Highly recommended

FOOD STYLE **INTERNATIONAL**
LICENSED **YES**
NON-SMOKING TABLES **NO**
WHEELCHAIR ACCESS **YES**
OPEN **SUN–SAT 9AM-MIDNIGHT**
PRICE **£(£)**

55 BC
128 Drymen Road, Bearsden   0141 942 7272

The affluent suburb of Bearsden is astonishingly poorly served by good restaurants so this curious establishment has to fly the flag almost unaided. The name presumably echoes the Roman Road round the corner. You have to enter via a pub. That presents a real obstacle to all but the bravest souls – walk past the slot machines to the tiny formal dining area at the back. Once there, you'll enjoy excellent cooking at fair prices, if you can get a table. The kitchen's strengths lie in preparing fresh local produce such as seafood, fish (several varieties), lamb, and beef. On the other hand, don't ignore the bar food as it turns out to be far superior to your usual gastropub fare. Butternut squash soup (a blackboard special) was thick, creamy and full of flavour. Cajun salmon with rice was tender, nicely seasoned and hard to fault. Desserts are interesting and the coffee good. Staff are pleasant, and strive hard to conceal their mild embarrassment at the eccentric surroundings.

Enjoy excellent cooking at fair prices, if you can get a table

FOOD STYLE **SCOTTISH**
LICENSED **YES**
NON-SMOKING TABLES **YES**
WHEELCHAIR ACCESS **YES**
OPEN **MON–SAT NOON-10PM**
      SUN 12.30PM-9PM (BAR MENU ONLY DURING DAY AND ON SUN–MON EVENINGS)
PRICE **££(£)**

FIREBIRD

1321 Argyle Street   0141 334 0594

A strangely crescent shaped dining area with an even stranger mural of a large non-human primate on the far wall, this café bar is hard to dislike. The tables are wooden yet comfortable enough, the high windows ensure plenty of light, and there are even some outside tables to which smokers ought to be confined in

This café bar is hard to dislike

summer but, annoyingly, aren't. The menu is fairly international and gets expensive if you delve too deeply into the main course section. Soups, sandwiches and other snacks are good value and reliable but the salads are a bit special with avocado, marinated olives and spinach cropping up unexpectedly. The great delicacy here is pizza, prepared expertly in a wood-fired stove and served with adventurous toppings. Everything looks and tastes as fresh and organic as claimed. The young staff, attired in (too casual?) jeans and tee shirts, cope valiantly with rush-hour pressure though there should be more of them. Beware of DJs at weekends.

FOOD STYLE **ITALIAN/INTERNATIONAL**
LICENSED **YES**
NON-SMOKING TABLES **YES**
WHEELCHAIR ACCESS **YES**
OPEN **SUN–THUR 11AM-10PM**
         FRI–SAT 11AM-10.30PM
PRICE **££**

GINGERHILL
1 Hillhead Street, Milngavie   0141 956 6515

The commuter suburb of Milngavie is hardly teeming with
good restaurants so the locals show their appreciation by
packing out Gingerhill on a regular basis. Finding the
place is the first challenge, negotiating the steep staircase the second. Once inside, you can relax as the
limited space has been ingeniously organised to banish
claustrophobia. Proprietor Alan Burns has maintained the
tradition of focusing on fresh local produce, mainly fish
and seafood, inventively grilled,
poached, peat-smoked or baked
in a variety of beguiling sauces
and dressings. There are meat
and vegetarian offerings on the
regularly changing menu but if
that doesn't suit you are free to

Locals show their appreciation by packing out Gingerhill on a regular basis

discuss with the staff any special requests or unorthodox
variants. Starters and desserts (if you get that far) are
equally memorable. The staff are eager to please and
seem genuinely proud of their efforts. The pace is
leisurely and that's just fine especially as the recently
acquired licence allows you to anticipate the pleasures
ahead with an aperitif in the lounge.

FOOD STYLE **FISH**
LICENSED **YES**
NON-SMOKING TABLES **YES**
WHEELCHAIR ACCESS **NO**
OPEN **WED–SUN 7-9.30PM**
PRICE **££(£)**

GRASSROOTS CAFE
93 St Georges Road   0141 333 0534

Glasgow is poorly served for good vegetarian restaurants so Grassroots does a roaring trade despite the awkward location. A recent refurbishment has improved the look of the place considerably though an assortment of ill-matching items of furniture ensures that it retains a kind of 1960s student-land character. The menu indicates what is vegetarian, vegan and gluten free and the blackboard specials (framed by fairy lights!) always contain something appetising. Excellent starters include vegetable soup, tempura and a range of unusual salads. They employ many Middle Eastern ingredients (felafel, hummus, couscous, haloumi, aubergine) though less exotic standbys such as sausages, burgers and pizzas (all strictly veggie of course) are in constant demand from the young clientele. Both starters and mains are fresh, tasty and filling, and arguably the desserts are even better. Innumerable varieties of coffee and tea are available. Curiously for an establishment that takes a strong line against GM and non-organic crops, smoking is tolerated. The world is indeed a strange place.

Blackboard specials always contain something appetising

FOOD STYLE **VEGETARIAN**
LICENSED **YES**
NON-SMOKING TABLES **YES**
WHEELCHAIR ACCESS **YES**
OPEN **MON–FRI 10AM-10PM**
        SAT–SUN 10AM-3.45PM, 5-10PM
PRICE **£**

HAUGH
5 Byres Road   0141 339 8511

Having changed its name from Arisaig and prior to that from the problematic Living Room, Haugh is a different kettle of fish – among other ingredients. The room is split into two, the first more of a cocktail bar though they'll let you eat here at lunchtime if you wish. The menu is deter-minedly Scottish but has been con-structed with imagination – haggis, oatmeal, venison and seaweed crop up in various guises. Early reports on the quality and quantity of the food were mixed but the kitchen seems to

Soups are wonderful for a Partick winter's day

have settled down nicely. Soups are wonderful for a Partick winter's day, the accompanying bread is crisp and fresh. Vegetables are gently cooked and even the chunky chips have a superior, non-soggy texture. Burgers and sausages are not as successful as their popularity with student diners suggests. Desserts are possibly the real strong point. Servers are well meaning if not always wholly effective.

FOOD STYLE **SCOTTISH**
LICENSED **YES**
NON-SMOKING TABLES **YES**
WHEELCHAIR ACCESS **YES**
OPEN **MON–SAT NOON-10PM**
       SUN 12.30-10PM.
PRICE **££**

ICHIBAN NOODLE CAFÉ
184 Dumbarton Road   0141 334 9222

Japanese food may not be to everyone's taste but this unusual eatery has won over sceptics in droves. The original Ichiban in the city centre (50 Queen Street, 0141 204 4200) has spawned a modernistic West End branch. The austere wooden bench seating can be forbidding at first but most rear ends will adjust quickly. The lunch deal comprises a main course and side dish for a relatively paltry sum (around £6) and the staff are happy to let you

The Japanese curry dishes are a revelation

share dishes, a procedure to be highly recommended. Portions are substantial and are presented with a variety of unpronounceable sauces. The Japanese curry dishes are a revelation, quite unlike their more pungent Indian counterparts. Even if you can't tell your ramen from your udon noodles, and sushi leaves you cold, you can hardly fail to enjoy the experience. Heated saki is the tipple of choice though there is a decent South African white that washes everything down perfectly. Look out for servers' electronic gadgets to record your order.

Highly recommended

FOOD STYLE **JAPANESE**
LICENSED **YES**
NON-SMOKING TABLES **YES**
WHEELCHAIR ACCESS **YES**
OPEN **MON–WED NOON-10PM**
     THUR–SAT NOON-11PM; SUN 1-10PM
PRICE **£(£)**

KEMBER & JONES
134 Byres Road   0141 337 3851

A combined deli and café, the K&J Fine Food Emporium has caused quite a stir on Byres Road – and that's no mean feat. The floor space is not vast and it gets pretty crowded as throngs of inquisitive shoppers wander the ground floor displays of kitchenware, Arran mustard and hand-made muesli (!) Such is the extraordinary popularity of the café that vacant seats are as gold dust at peak times. What is the attraction? In a word, quality. The cheeses, salads, vegetables, baking and meats are fresh, tasty and beautifully presented on impressive platters. These are not cheap, upwards of £7 a dish, but they are sizeable and you may feel inclined to share. If coffee and cake suffices, you have a dilemma – how can you possibly choose between unrivalled home-made scones and jam, and lemon polenta cake topped with brambles? As expected, coffee and tea are outstanding though you might find a glass of the excellent house red more alluring.

What is the attraction? In a word, quality

FOOD STYLE **INTERNATIONAL**
LICENSED **YES**
NON-SMOKING TABLES **YES**
WHEELCHAIR ACCESS **YES**
OPEN **MON–SAT 9AM-7PM**
      SUN 10AM–6PM
PRICE **££**

KONAKI
920 Sauchiehall Street   0141 342 4010

This modest looking taverna feels authentically Greek from the moment you step inside, an impression aided by the unobtrusive yet ethnically appropriate soundtrack. The front section is small and quite cramped but there are lots more tables at the back. The menu has all the usual Greek dishes – ask about the changing soup of the day – though you can opt for straightforward salad, pasta or omelette (expertly done, by the way). The chargrilled

Under no circumstances should you skip dessert

chicken souvlaki is rightly popular, and is served with plentiful rice and salad. Retsina is an obvious accompaniment but why not abandon inhibitions and order one of the less familiar but surprisingly palatable Cretan white wines? Under no circumstances should you skip dessert. All are wonderful, including the strawberry cheesecake, but the kataifi and baklava are nothing short of sensational. Coffee is good but the lemon tea is better. Fantastic value lunch. There are occasional Greek party nights if you are so inclined.

Highly recommended

FOOD STYLE **GREEK**
LICENSED **YES**
NON-SMOKING TABLES **YES**
WHEELCHAIR ACCESS **YES**
OPEN **MON–SAT NOON-2.30PM, 5-11PM**
      SUN 5-11PM
PRICE **££**

MIMMOS BISTRO

31 Ashton Lane   0141 339 1848

Remember Mitchell's on this site? This Italian successor bears little resemblance although the bright pink (or is it orange?) paintwork has been retained. The room is tiny and tables are consequently cheek-by-jowl, a major drawback if you are looking for privacy or if your selfish neighbour decides to light up. Everything else is delightful, though, including the prices – the superb value set lunch at £6.50 for two courses (from an admittedly very limited choice) is almost miraculous.

If either penne castalinga or lasagne is on the menu, no need to hesitate

And the food is the genuine article, from the thick, piping hot minestrone, through satisfying pastas, to the best espresso coffee in this highly competitive lane. If either penne castalinga or lasagne is on the menu, no need to hesitate. Service is rapid and portions vast. The house white (at £8.50 a bottle) is more than adequate but drink slowly or you'll never make it down the steep staircase at the end of your meal.

FOOD STYLE **ITALIAN**
LICENSED **YES**
NON-SMOKING TABLES **NO**
WHEELCHAIR ACCESS **NO**
OPEN **MON-SUN 12 NOON-10PM**
PRICE **££**

MOTHER INDIA

28 Westminster Terrace, Sauchiehall Street
0141 221 1663

When it opened around a decade ago, Mother India broke the mould of Glasgow's curry houses by focusing on truly authentic Indian cuisine subtly adapted to meet local needs. The setting is less stylish than the food, though the upstairs room, with its long wooden tables, velvet curtains and elaborate lighting, is more appealing than the ground floor. The menu is relatively short but packed with innovation. This is serious, meticulous Indian cooking of a rare standard. Aubergine fritters are terrific for starters, and any of the fish or lamb dishes maintain the high quality. Cumin, cardamon and garlic are amongst the wide range of Punjabi and other spices that tease the palate. Try to engage the apparently uncommunicative staff in a conversation about their favourite subject – food – and you should be amply rewarded. Vegetarians need have no fears and the kitchen will rise to the challenge of most individual requirements. Though now licensed, the BYOB tradition survives.

This is serious, meticulous Indian cooking of a rare standard

Highly recommended

FOOD STYLE **INDIAN**
LICENSED **YES**
NON-SMOKING TABLES **No**
WHEELCHAIR ACCESS **YES**
OPEN **MON–TUE 5.30-10.30PM**
      WED–THUR NOON-2PM, 5.30-10.30PM
      FRI NOON-2PM, 5.30-11PM
      SAT 1-11PM; SUN 4.30-10PM
PRICE **££**

MOTHER INDIA'S CAFÉ
1355 Argyle Street   0141 339 9145

This site seems problematic these days, perhaps due to the (temporary) closure of the Kelvingrove Museum opposite. This offshoot of the Mother India empire may have struck the right note, after a reportedly bumpy start, with an innovative and thus presumably high risk venture. The idea is to merge two current Glaswegian passions – tapas and curries. What you get here is thali – a kind of Indian tapas. There are around forty of these small and modestly priced dishes ranging from pakora to chicken karahi. You are encouraged to order several and share. Although a reasonable wine list is available, draught Kingfisher may be the wiser choice. The really inspired feature is to serve a range of delightfully unfamiliar Indian sweets on a multi-layered platter along with tea or coffee. This can backfire as customers who haven't ordered a beverage glower jealously at those who have. Time will tell whether this brave experiment has paid off.

The idea is to merge two current Glaswegian passions – tapas and curries

FOOD STYLE **INDIAN**
LICENSED **YES**
NON-SMOKING TABLES **YES**
WHEELCHAIR ACCESS **YES**
OPEN **MON–FRI NOON-2PM, 5-10PM**
     SAT–SUN 11AM-10PM
PRICE **£(£)**

NO. SIXTEEN
16 Byres Road   0141 339 2544

Despite several personnel changes, this minuscule place has retained its high reputation for freshness, innovation and quality. You sense that everyone concerned is striving for excellence and it shows. How do they do it? Simple, really. When you combine outstanding cooking with deft presentation and polished service, you've made a terrific start. Add an extra, crucial ingredient – good value – and you have a winner. The ingredients are eclectic with a strong Scottish accent, including outstanding fish and game. Desserts – arguably the best in the west – are not to be missed. Wines are carefully chosen though a little pricey. Take your time and savour the experience – you know you are in good hands. And the set lunch (around £11) is a remarkable bargain. The surroundings are quaint and definitely not for the claustrophobic, especially if you are directed to the vertiginous mezzanine floor. Don't be deterred. No. 16 edges ever closer to the number one slot in the West End.

Take your time and savour the experience – you know you are in good hands

Highly recommended

FOOD STYLE **SCOTTISH**
LICENSED **YES**
NON-SMOKING TABLES **YES**
WHEELCHAIR ACCESS **NO**
OPEN **MON–SAT NOON-2.30PM, 5.30-10PM
SUN 12.30-4PM, 5.30-9.30PM**
PRICE **££(£)**

ONE DEVONSHIRE GARDENS

One Devonshire Gardens   **0141 339 2001**

Amaryllis is no more, but this stately luxury hotel is trying hard to recover its reputation for gourmet dining by opening a branch of Room (of Leeds fame) in the former Ramsay shrine. How that pans out remains unclear but, main restaurant aside, ODG has at least one more ace up its sleeve – afternoon tea served in a beautiful Victorian lounge (at No 5). For a reasonable set price (£15 per person) you get a sensational traditional tea with sandwiches and cakes of unrivalled quality in

The cakes are glorious, the freshly baked scones melt in the mouth

these parts. If you have preferences for particular types of sandwich fillings, the staff will accommodate you if they have advance notice. Platter after platter arrives in almost theatrical fashion. The cakes are glorious, the freshly baked scones melt in the mouth, the eclairs are intoxicating, the truffles astonishing. Everything is washed down with copious quantities of perfectly brewed tea served immaculately from endlessly refilled silverware. Take your time, gorge yourself and stagger into the street utterly stuffed – but ecstatic. Sheer joy. Remember to book in advance.

FOOD STYLE **SCOTTISH**
LICENSED **YES**
NON-SMOKING TABLES **NO**
WHEELCHAIR ACCESS **YES**
OPEN **MON-SUN 2-4.30PM**
PRICE **££(£)**

ORAN MOR

371 Great Western Road   0141 357 6200

As Scotland becomes increasingly secular, a large number of empty churches litter the urban landscape and new uses have to be found for them. Following the lead of Cottier's up the road, the owners of this imposing corner building have invested huge sums in creating another entertainment and cultural centre. Oranmor is Gaelic for 'great melody' and music certainly features strongly in the events programme. The banqueting hall seats 400 and is

Initial reports are promising

justly famous for its ceiling painting by Alasdair Gray. The main bar is a huge room that already attracts droves of students, academics, business folk and local celebs. Just off this room is a smallish, rather austere bistro serving a limited selection of mainly Scottish dishes at intermediate prices. Initial reports are promising. A more upmarket brasserie had yet to materialise at the time of writing. One early blunder – placing a couple of sinister-looking heavies so prominently at the front door is hardly indicative of a warm welcome.

FOOD STYLE **SCOTTISH**
LICENSED **YES**
NON-SMOKING TABLES **YES**
WHEELCHAIR ACCESS **YES**
OPEN **SUN–SAT NOON-10PM (PROVISIONAL)**
PRICE **££**

SHISH MAHAL
60-68 Park Road   0141 339 8256

Celebrating 40 years in the West End, the appeal of the Shish transcends the generation gap. The physical space isn't large, yet comfort and elegance abound. The crisp white tablecloths and napkins (unfolded ceremoniously on your lap) tell you instantly that much has changed since the 1960s despite claims to being 'unspoilt by progress'. The staff are pleasant if rather subdued, generating a slightly over-reverential atmosphere. Don't miss the exquisite pakora – potato and cauliflower, aubergine and mushroom are all pleasing to both palate and digestion. Go easy on the starters, though, for one portion is more than enough for two. Koftas, biryanis, tikka masalas – they're all there and you won't go far wrong choosing virtually at random. The boiled rice is fluffy and light. Naans are suitably massive. Vegetarians are spoilt for choice in almost every section of the menu. Prices are mostly reasonable though dinner will cost you about double the excellent value lunch.

Don't miss the exquisite pakora

FOOD STYLE **INDIAN**
LICENSED **YES**
NON-SMOKING TABLES **YES**
WHEELCHAIR ACCESS **YES**
OPEN **MON–THUR NOON-2PM, 5-11PM**
      FRI–SAT NOON-11.30PM; SUN 5-11PM
PRICE **££**

STAZIONE

1051 Great Western Road   0141 576 7576

JJ Burnet's superb 1896 Kelvinside railway station has been brilliantly converted into a bar and two restaurants. Stazione, the more modest of the pair, is located on the ground floor in the old ticketing hall. The menu is described as Mediterranean, though the Italian tradition dominates. Especially nice touches are the small bowl of olives on your table and a tiny glass of complimentary Kir. The set lunch, at £11.75 for two courses may look

Even haddock fried in batter with chips is a great success

expensive but it really isn't given the combination of quality and quantity. The dishes may be unsophisticated, the presentation unpretentious and the service informal but the end results are surprisingly good. Even haddock fried in batter with chips is a great success, as are the more exotic Asian spiced chicken and Statzione Caesar salad. Desserts are somewhat daunting – the bowl of rhubarb crumble would feed a family – and you may opt for one of an impressive range of coffees instead. The upstairs Lux, under the same management, is altogether more ambitious and this is reflected in its prices.

FOOD STYLE **ITALIAN/INTERNATIONAL**
LICENSED **YES**
NON-SMOKING TABLES **NO**
WHEELCHAIR ACCESS **YES**
OPEN **MON–FRI NOON-2.30PM, 5.30PM TILL LATE; SAT–SUN NOON TILL LATE**
PRICE **££**

STRAVAIGIN

28 Gibson Street   0141 334 2665

This award winning restaurant looks rather nondescript from the outside and not much better within. The ground floor café bar has the advantage of light and air while the (smoke free) basement is where you'll encounter those intent on making more of an occasion of their visit. Colin Clydesdale and his team have adopted an adventurous philosophy of giving fresh local produce an international (mainly oriental) treatment and the

Lemon and thyme roast mushrooms may convert you to vegetarianism

results vary from noble failures to spectacular triumphs. If you've ever wondered what squid salad with capers and smoked paprika tastes like, here's your chance. They do a lovely Thai green curry with steamed rice, and the lemon and thyme roast mushrooms may convert you to vegetarianism. If all this is too exotic, the fish and chips are renowned, as are the haggis (including a veggie version) and game dishes. Don't neglect the impossibly alluring desserts – Belgian chocolate and walnut brownies or ginger beer ice cream, for example. Staff mostly cope well but you may need to be patient at peak times.

FOOD STYLE **SCOTTISH**
LICENSED **YES**
NON-SMOKING TABLES **YES**
WHEELCHAIR ACCESS **NO**
OPEN **TUE–THUR 5-11PM**
      FRI–SUN NOON-2.30PM, 5-11PM
      CLOSED MON
PRICE **££(£)**

STRAVAIGIN 2

8 Ruthven Lane   0141 334 7165

The lanes off Byres Road contain some real treasures and here is one. An offshoot of its very different namesake in Gibson Street, this delightful bistro often outshines its sibling. The dining area straddles two floors, the upstairs loft area being the more spacious and light. The menu is truly extraordinary, spanning continents and styles but with a pronounced Scottish accent. If Louisiana crab cakes or mussels with coriander don't appeal, what about free range duck egg on chapati, or a common-or-garden ostrich burger and chips? This may sound gimmicky – and it is – but relax, the food is terrific. Ingredients are fresh, the cooking refined and the presentation polished. Portions are substantial, the staff helpful and the setting comfortable. What else could you want? Consistency? You've got it. Good value for money? That's thrown in too. Trust me – you are unlikely to find a better meal at sensible prices in upper Byres Road.

> *The menu is truly extraordinary, spanning continents and styles*

Highly recommended

FOOD STYLE **INTERNATIONAL**
LICENSED **YES**
NON-SMOKING TABLES **YES**
WHEELCHAIR ACCESS **YES**
OPEN **MON–FRI NOON-11PM**
       SAT–SUN 11AM-11PM
PRICE **££**

TRATTORIA TREVI
526 Great Western Road   0141 334 3262

One of life's welcome constants, Trevi is a haven of Mediterranean warmth among the grey tenements of Kelvinbridge. The room is tiny, its walls and ceiling copiously adorned with amusing football memorabilia. The wooden seats are functional rather than comfortable. The standard menu arguably lacks originality – fans of pasta, pizza and risotto won't complain – but there's nothing bland about the textures and flavours of the food. Don't overlook the changing blackboard specials about which the voluble staff won't hesitate to offer advice. The cooking (by the owner's mother) is traditional, almost rustic Italian in nature, employing carefully selected, fresh ingredients. Soup and fish dishes are especially satisfying but almost everything has a homely, authentic feel. Both white and red house wines are safe choices. The range of desserts is limited. Coffee is slightly disappointing, served without mints. Outside tables have been spotted in summer. Set lunch and pre-theatre deals keep prices under control. A veritable West End gem.

Trevi is a haven of Mediterranean warmth among the grey tenements of Kelvinbridge

FOOD STYLE **ITALIAN**
LICENSED **YES**
NON-SMOKING TABLES **No**
WHEELCHAIR ACCESS **No**
OPEN **MON–THUR NOON-2.30PM, 5-11PM**
      FRI NOON-2.30PM, 6-11PM
      SAT 6-11PM SUN 5-11PM
PRICE **££**

TWO FAT LADIES
88 Dumbarton Road   0141 339 1944

When this tiny seafood restaurant first opened several years ago, it created something of a sensation. Thereafter it has had a chequered career but its reputation is on the up once more. The front of house area is perhaps a little too close to the kitchen, though the staff welcome prying eyes. Furnishings are simple but effective. The walls are covered in original paintings of variable quality. Curiously quiet at midday – despite a superb value lunch menu

The high standard is maintained all the way to coffee served with delicious chocolat

– it fills quickly most evenings. Meat and poultry dishes are more visible these days but they still do a mean bream. An air of quiet confidence informs everything that occurs here and you will soon discover why. All the ingredients are fresh, the food lovingly prepared and carefully presented. Sauces are particularly fine, subtly flavoured and ideally matched to the protein on your plate. The house white (Chenin Blanc) is a worthy accompaniment. The high standard is maintained all the way to coffee served with delicious chocolate.

Highly recommended

FOOD STYLE **FISH**
LICENSED **YES**
NON-SMOKING TABLES **NO**
WHEELCHAIR ACCESS **YES**
OPEN **MON– SAT NOON-3PM, 5-10PM**
         SUN 5-10PM
PRICE **££(£)**

UBIQUITOUS CHIP
12 Ashton Lane   0141 334 5007

The Grand Old Lady of Ashton Lane (an increasingly lively student-dominated cluster of bars and restaurants) has remained close to the top of anyone's list of great Glasgow restaurants for about three decades. The photogenic, jungle-like indoor courtyard is unique though the trickling fountain may play havoc with sensitive bladders! The menu is worth studying with care. It contains an impressive array of classic Scottish dishes (try white fish, haggis or venison – all consistently memorable) along with some weirder offerings (fried seaweed, shark) that will amuse out-of-town visitors. The wine list is legendary for both its content and length. The Chip has its detractors but its capacity for survival tells you that Ronald Clydesdale is doing something right. Agreed, the prices are high and the portion sizes sometimes disappoint but there's a special atmosphere here that won't let you down. This is a great venue for graduation lunches or other special occasions.

This is a great venue for graduation lunches or other special occasions

FOOD STYLE **SCOTTISH**
LICENSED **YES**
NON-SMOKING TABLES **NO**
WHEELCHAIR ACCESS **YES**
OPEN **MON– SAT NOON-2.30PM, 5.30-11PM
        SUN 12.30-3PM, 6.30-11PM**
PRICE **£££**

The WEE CURRY SHOP

29 Ashton Lane   0141 357 5280

The cross-cultural name refers to the room not the food. The original, and similarly microscopic, version of this can be found in the less salubrious Garnethill district at 7 Buccleuch Street (0141 353 0777). The Ashton Lane branch is another offshoot of Mother India and is up against tough local competition but seems to be holding up well. The tables are necessarily packed close together so you can have endless fun eavesdropping on your neighbour. Because you can't swing a popadom in the kitchen, the choice is more limited than in many Indian restaurants but they get by remarkably well. Well-filled, mildly spiced vegetable pakora or aubergine fritters with chilli dip followed by any of the chicken, lamb or vegetarian dishes will keep most curry fans contented. The knowledgeable staff will advise on sauce strengths. Portions are ample, prices are lowish, and the set lunch is fantastic value at £6.50 (though even that is steep compared to Buccleuch Street where they charge less than a fiver!).

Any of the chicken, lamb or vegetarian dishes will keep most curry fans contented

FOOD STYLE **INDIAN**
LICENSED **YES**
NON-SMOKING TABLES **YES**
WHEELCHAIR ACCESS **No**
OPEN **MON–THUR 12.30-2.30PM, 5.30-10.30PM**
      FRI 12.30-2.30PM, 5.30-11PM
      SAT 12.30-11PM
      SUN 3-11PM
PRICE **£(£)**

CITY CENTRE

The City Centre comprises the main shopping, entertainment and commercial districts. The famous Sauchiehall Street meanders from the top end of Buchanan Street (at the Royal Concert Hall) westwards all the way to the University. Most of the theatres, cinemas and art galleries are to be found around the central and eastern part of Sauchiehall Street. Buchanan Street contains the large Buchanan Galleries mall and the renowned Princes Square shopping complex (Buchanan Street subway). There is another shopping precinct (the St Enoch Centre) at the lower end of Buchanan Street at its junction with the hugely popular Argyle Street (St Enoch subway). Due to the grid system of streets, finding your way around shouldn't pose too many problems – if you have a map!

ARTHOUSE GRILL
129 Bath Street   0141 572 6002

If you've ever wondered what a 'boutique hotel' is, have a wander around the Arthouse Hotel. An impressively refurbished townhouse, it positively oozes twenty-first century sophistication. The staff are attentive and professional, and radiate a calm and fortunately well-founded confidence in their abilities. The atmosphere is far from oppressive, nevertheless, and they're perfectly happy to welcome children.

Positively oozes twenty-first century sophistication

The menu is fairly global, with a strong Japanese tendency that comes to the fore in the Teppanyaki bar. Though there are outstanding meat and vegetarian options, the kitchen excels at fish and seafood: likely offerings include smoked salmon, lobster and asparagus terrine, scallops with Arran mustard, and pan-fried red snapper with pine nut coulis. Desserts are as stylish as the décor – dark chocolate pot with meringue and berries could only be created by someone on the staff who clearly knows a thing or two about life's priorities. Look out for the waterfall right in the centre of the main stairwell.

FOOD STYLE **INTERNATIONAL/JAPANESE**
LICENSED **YES**
NON-SMOKING TABLES **NO**
WHEELCHAIR ACCESS **NO**
OPEN **MON–SUN 7AM-11PM**
PRICE **££(£)**

La BONNE AUBERGE

161 West Nile Street   0141 352 8310

La Bonne Auberge, on the ground floor of the Holiday Inn, does a roaring trade in rushed concert-goers and with good reason. This has the feel of a real French brasserie with a particularly comfortable bar area if you can find a seat. The fixed price menu (about £15 for two courses until 7.30pm, rising a couple pounds thereafter) is one of the best, though not the cheapest, in the vicinity. Soups are excellent and the other starters (parfait of chicken liver, oriental style vegetable salad) are too enticing to overlook. Main courses, such as tandoori spiced hot smoked salmon and chargrilled rib-eye steak, are as appetising as they sound, artfully cooked and beautifully presented. If you're prepared to pay for the full evening menu (over £20 for two courses), you'll find more ambitious dishes including seafood, beef, duck and ostrich. Wine bottles start at around £13 and go all the way up to Dom Perignon at £98. The staff are pleasant enough to merit the 'optional' 10% service charge.

> *Has the feel of a real French brasserie*

FOOD STYLE **FRENCH**
LICENSED **YES**
NON-SMOKING TABLES **YES**
WHEELCHAIR ACCESS **YES**
OPEN **MON–THUR NOON-2.15PM, 5-10PM;**
    FRI–SAT NOON-2.15PM, 5-10.30PM;
    SUN NOON-2.15PM, 5-9PM
PRICE **£££**

BRIAN MAULE AT CHARDON D'OR

176 West Regent Street   0141 248 3801

Those who remember the old Brasserie on this site won't recognise the place. It's now a rather understated, sleek and modernistic room with a polished wooden floor and glass panels. The BM logo tells you that self-esteem is not a problem for Brian Maule, formerly of Michelin-starred Le Gavroche. That quiet confidence permeates everything here, the tranquil setting, unhurried service and a menu that is mercifully gimmick-free.

First-rate classical French cooking albeit embellished with favourite Scottish ingredients

This is first-rate classical French cooking albeit embellished with favourite Scottish ingredients. Unusually, the set menu doesn't insult the diner's taste in food. Cappuccino of creamed potato and leek has a velvety texture on the tongue, and fillet of salmon on a bed of leeks with a light champagne sauce is just as beguiling. Any of the fish dishes are expertly executed and there are good reports of pork rillettes. Crème brûlée, like the rest of the meal, is judged to perfection, but you are really in luck if any apricot trifle topped with vanilla yoghurt is left. All very impressive, though standards of service slip occasionally, presumably when the boss isn't about.

Highly recommended

FOOD STYLE **FRENCH**
LICENSED **YES**
NON-SMOKING TABLES **YES**
WHEELCHAIR ACCESS **NO**
OPEN **MON–FRI NOON-2.30PM, 6-10PM;**
      SAT 6-10PM; CLOSED SUN
PRICE **£££**

The BUTTERY

652 Argyle Street   0141 221 8188

Once known as 'The Shandon Buttery', this much loved
Glasgow institution traces its pedigree back to 1869.
Saved from demolition in the 1960s, it looks somewhat
forlorn perched at the end of a cul-de-sac near the M8.
Entirely non-smoking (congratulations!) except for the
small oyster bar, the décor is frankly astonishing, Gothic in
style with impressive wood panelling throughout, beautiful stained glass and charming artefacts in every corner.

*Very special,
very enjoyable
and very
expensive*

The menu is firmly Scottish, though
with occasional continental and even
oriental forays. Each dish is lovingly
described – listen to this: confit shank
of Perthshire lamb pressed between
potato layers with a sun blushed toma-
to and black olive salad and winter vegetable casserole;
honeyed roulade of root vegetables bound in Savoy cab-
bage; Ochil Venison on a pear and sultana mash with red
wine and onions. Desserts are legendary. Chef Deans is
clearly a master and well worthy of his numerous awards.
Service is immaculate and attentive. Very special, very
enjoyable and very expensive (except for the set lunch, a
bargain at £16).

Highly recommended

FOOD STYLE **SCOTTISH**
LICENSED **YES**
NON-SMOKING TABLES **YES**
WHEELCHAIR ACCESS **No**
OPEN **TUE–THUR NOON-2PM, 7-10PM; FRI NOON-2PM,
6-10PM; SAT 6-10PM; CLOSED SUN–MON**
PRICE **£££**

CHINATOWN

42 New City Road   0141 353 0037

If you have trouble finding this one, you're not alone! Its obscure location hasn't dented the fortunes of Chinatown. In part, that's because it is situated in the nearest thing Glasgow has to a Chinese quarter in the multicultural borderland between Cowcaddens and Garnethill. On entering the dining room, the visual impression is startling – huge picture windows, a giant crystal chandelier, a massive fish tank. These dramatic features all but dwarf the prettily decorated tables. An encouragingly large proportion of the diners are Chinese, testifying to the authenticity of the food. The menu is lengthy and choosing is far from easy. The dim sum is legendary so that's a good starting point. Other recommendations include shark's fin soup, duck, sliced fish and a range of exotic seafood concoctions the likes of which you are unlikely to encounter elsewhere. Buffet evenings are joyously self-indulgent occasions. The extensive wine list adds to the bewildering number of decisions to be made. Service is efficient and closely attentive at all times.

Buffet evenings are joyously self-indulgent occasions

FOOD STYLE **CHINESE**
LICENSED **YES**
NON-SMOKING TABLES **NO**
WHEELCHAIR ACCESS **YES**
OPEN **MON–SUN NOON-11.30PM**
PRICE **££**

D'ARCYS

Princes Square, Buchanan Street   0141 226 4309

Unaccountably underrated by food buffs – perhaps because of its location in a shopping mall – D'Arcys has been around for many years and continues to pull in the crowds, including families with extremely young children, so they're doing something right. The seating area looks enormous but that is partly because many of the tables have invaded the main courtyard. The more secluded inner sanctum feels more like a proper restaurant.

Unaccountably underrated by food buffs

The furnishings are vaguely art deco, the walls adorned with decent (presumably reproduction) paintings. Staff greet you with a smile and present you with a pricey à la carte menu, though a set meal is available at specified times. Salads, pastas and fish dishes are particularly successful, and even the most basic sounding snacks are carefully prepared and presented. The small dessert section gives pause for thought – go for sticky toffee pudding, one of the best in the city. Strong filter coffee comes with a disappointingly bland biscuit.

FOOD STYLE **INTERNATIONAL**
LICENSED **YES**
NON-SMOKING TABLES **YES**
WHEELCHAIR ACCESS **YES**
OPEN **MON–SAT 11.30AM-10PM**
     SUN NOON-6PM
PRICE **££**

DI MAGGIO'S CITY CENTRE
21 Royal Exchange Square   0141 248 2111

Royal Exchange Square can seem almost continental in semi-decent weather thanks to the civilising presence of clusters of outdoor tables attached to cafés and restaurants, including Di Maggio's flagship branch that has about 80 al fresco seats in the square. The narrow entrance, negotiated via a revolving door, conceals an oblong room that seems to stretch for miles. This is modern

All the dishes have stood the test of time

art deco at its flashiest with mirrors, spotlights and contemporary art. The menu is standard for the chain, and impressive it is too once you've accepted the populist presentation. All the dishes have stood the test of time pretty well, pizzas being exemplary, pastas not far behind. Of the house wines, stick to the red (Merlot) though you might be tempted by the extraordinarily good value house champagne (Paul Herard £19.95). Try chocolate fudge cake or ice cream for dessert. Although child friendly, tots seem to be less in evidence at this branch. Don't wander in on a Saturday lunchtime unless you enjoy queuing.

FOOD STYLE **ITALIAN**
LICENSED **YES**
NON-SMOKING TABLES **YES**
WHEELCHAIR ACCESS **YES**
OPEN **MON–SAT NOON-MIDNIGHT**
       SUN 12.30-10.30PM
PRICE **££**

The DOOCOT CAFÉ

The Lighthouse, 11 Mitchell Lane   0141 221 1821

Doocot is the local vernacular for 'dove cot' though the avian connection is rather tenuous. The real point of coming here is to see the building, a refurbished Mackintosh masterpiece that functions as an architectural centre. The café is on the fifth floor and extremely appealing it is too with its circular white tables, Scandinavian-style chairs and pleasantly subdued background music. The black-uniformed waitresses are pleasant if only semi-competent. The menu is short and unexceptional – soups, salads, sandwiches, pasta, ice cream, all well presented on superior crockery. Coffee is better than average and the tea comes in a pot. You're under no obligation to eat a full meal – there are tempting scones, cakes and ice creams should you wish to indulge yourself or your younger charges. The bar will rise to a bottle of champagne if you're in celebratory mood. A bright, relaxing, child friendly place that offers soothing respite from lower Buchanan Street.

A bright, relaxing, child friendly place

FOOD STYLE **INTERNATIONAL**
LICENSED **YES**
NON-SMOKING TABLES **YES**
WHEELCHAIR ACCESS **YES**
OPEN **MON–SAT 11.30AM-5PM**
     SUN NOON-5PM
PRICE **£**

ÉTAIN

Springfield Court, Princes Square   0141 225 5630

The enigmatic name (meaning pewter) sets the tone for this discreetly situated Conran 'fine-dining' establishment adjoining Zinc. The room is large, square and severely formal though with much daytime natural light from the window that comprises an entire wall. White linen table cloths and uniformed waiters reinforce the sense of unrestrained grandeur. The smiling staff do their best (despite the automatic service charge) to put you at ease. The for-

Fresh local produce is framed in intriguingly quirky flavours

midable menu warrants careful scrutiny. Head chef Geoffrey Smeddle wouldn't be trying to impress the city that has spawned at least a couple of Britain's most famous celebrity chefs, would he? Whatever the intention, the end results are certainly memorable. Fresh local produce is framed in intriguingly quirky flavours such as fennel, pomegranate, juniper and beetroot. Elaborately dressed seafood gets star billing though there are plenty more mainstream options. How to choose from this extraordinary panoply of gourmet goodies? Just order the six-course Epicurean Menu (£35) and enjoy. It's a special occasion after all.

FOOD STYLE **FRENCH**
LICENSED **YES**
NON-SMOKING TABLES **YES**
WHEELCHAIR ACCESS **YES**
OPEN **MON–FRI NOON-2.30PM, 7-11PM**
      SAT 7-11PM; SUN NOON-3PM
PRICE **£££**

FRATELLI SARTI

121 Bath Street   0141 204 0440

The last time I counted, there were three Sarti branches
in addition to this basement restaurant, the others being
at 133 Wellington Street (though this is really just the deli
part of Bath Street) and at 42 Renfield Street (tel: 0141
572 7000) and 404 Sauchiehall Street (tel: 0141 572
3360) where you'll have to climb a steep staircase. All are
regularly packed with aficionados so unsurprisingly the
service can be erratic at peak times. In the best Italian

The range and invention of the dishes is remarkable

tradition, there are red chequered
tablecloths, an open kitchen and olives
on the tables. The management is
clearly serious about the quality of the
food and drink – you won't go wrong
with either the house white or red. The
range and invention of the dishes is remarkable, with the
Tuscan specialities especially noteworthy. True, they don't
always quite live up to their aspirations – a pizza margari-
ta at the Sauchiehall Street branch arrived overcooked
and chewy. Soups and desserts are both reliable and
occasionally brilliant.

FOOD STYLE **ITALIAN**
LICENSED **YES**
NON-SMOKING TABLES **YES**
WHEELCHAIR ACCESS **NO**
OPEN **MON–THUR 8AM-10.30PM**
　　　FRI–SAT 8AM-11PM
　　　SUN NOON-10.30PM
PRICE **££**

GAMBA

225A West George Street   0141 572 0899

Winner of a slew of fine dining awards, subject of numerous rave reviews and the epicentre of a growing empire of
restaurants in the city, Gamba has become a well-established gourmet hot-spot. The fish is freshly delivered and
cooked in virtuoso fashion,
employing a variety of internation-
ally inspired approaches, by chef
Derek Marshall. Fish soup is exemplary. Steamed halibut comes in a
sealed parcel containing ginger,
onion and other delicate flavours. The kitchen's skills
extend to desserts too, judging by the memorable cheesecake and a terrific chocolate sponge. The adulation is far
from universal, however, with some disgruntled diners
muttering about inflated prices and marketing hype.
Prices are certainly high. À la carte starters are in the
region of £8-10 with main courses about double that, and
you can spend over £100 on a bottle of wine. You can keep
costs predictable by selecting the fixed price dinner (three
courses plus coffee) for £35. The lunch and pre-theatre
menus are relative give-aways (£16-£18) though you may
have to eat quickly – the latter is confined to 5-6.15pm.
Put this one on your short list for a special occasion.

*Gamba has
become a
well-established
gourmet hot-spot*

Highly recommended

FOOD STYLE **FISH**
LICENSED **YES**
NON-SMOKING TABLES **YES**
WHEELCHAIR ACCESS **NO**
OPEN **MON–SAT NOON-2.30PM, 5-10.30PM
CLOSED SUN**
PRICE **£££**

MALMAISON

278 West George Street   0141 572 1001

The Malmaison Hotel may be part of a chain but doesn't feel like it. The building is architecturally famous having been originally a church designed by Alexander 'Greek' Thomson. You approach the brasserie via a spiral staircase that leads to the smart Champagne Bar that will serve you snacks and hot drinks as well as a bottle of bubbly. Sink into a comfortable armchair and enjoy an unusual scene that is illuminated by natural light during the day and flickering candles in the evening. The room has a subdued yet clearly Parisian atmosphere. The menu changes regularly and is beautifully constructed. The cooking is highly accomplished, every dish immaculately presented, and you can be confident of the quality of the wine. Desserts are a real treat – indulge yourself with pear tart tatin with Chantilly Cream. Nothing on the à la carte menu is cheap – summer minestrone with pesto is £4.75, fillet of cod £12.95, rib-eye steak £23.95 – so the set lunch at £10.95 looks a bargain.

The room has a subdued yet clearly Parisian atmosphere

FOOD STYLE **FRENCH**
LICENSED **YES**
NON-SMOKING TABLES **YES**
WHEELCHAIR ACCESS **YES**
OPEN **MON– SUN NOON-2.30PM, 5.30-10.30PM**
PRICE **£££**

MINSKYS
Hilton Hotel, 1 William St   0141 204 5555

The main restaurant in the Hilton is Cameron's, an impressively formal Scottish-French affair that has won plaudits over the years. But the real treasure is the more relaxed Minskys, a mock New York style deli that you access via the back of the lobby. A masterpiece of deception, you will hardly believe it only opened a few years ago. The old sepia photographs of the Minsky family (are they real?) on the walls, combined with the shiny wooden table-tops, enhance the pseudo-historic ethos of the place. Despite its American connections, the food is actually about as British as you can get. The self-service buffet is exceptional and great value. Go easy on the starters or you'll deprive yourself of the joys of the carvery, where succulent slabs of roast beef compete for your attention with fish, poultry and masses of fresh vegetables and salads. If you have room, the desserts are outstanding. Finish with coffee and mints.

The self-service buffet is exceptional and great value

Highly recommended

FOOD STYLE **BRITISH/SCOTTISH**
LICENSED **YES**
NON-SMOKING TABLES **YES**
WHEELCHAIR ACCESS **YES**
OPEN **MON–FRI 6.30AM-11PM**
       SAT–SUN 7AM-11PM
PRICE **££(£)**

PAPINGO

104 Bath Street   0141 332 6678

Numerous bars, cafés and restaurants have sprouted along both sides of Bath Street though the casual visitor would scarcely notice. That's because so many are below street level and are inherently claustrophobic. Papingo (meaning parrot in Scots, apparently) manages to avoid this through the clever use of lighting and a tastefully pale colour scheme that cleverly offsets the low ceiling. Owned by Alan Tomkins, of Gamba, and chairman of the

You expect high standards of cooking and presentation and that's exactly what you get

Glasgow restaurateurs association, you expect high standards of cooking and presentation and that's exactly what you get with uncanny consistency. The menu changes every few weeks and tends to reiterate tried and tested dishes such as fish soup with mussels, chicken liver pate, fillet of sea bass, spiced salmon and roast duck. Some main course prices will make you wince (roast rack of lamb £16.95, fillet of Angus Rossini £19.95) so you may veer towards the excellent vegetarian options, the set lunch (three courses for under £10) or slightly more expensive pre-theatre meal.

FOOD STYLE **SCOTTISH**
LICENSED **YES**
NON-SMOKING TABLES **YES**
WHEELCHAIR ACCESS **NO**
OPEN **MON–SAT NOON-2.30PM, 5-10.30PM**
     SUN 5-10PM
PRICE **£££**

PAVAROTTI TRATTORIA
91 Cambridge Street   0141 332 9713

There's an indefinably eccentric ethos to this intimate little place. Perhaps the slightly self-parodying features such as mock terracotta villa roof jutting from one wall, or the continuous operatic soundtrack, are responsible.

Ideally situated for local theatres, it has long specialised in rapidly served, low cost pre-theatre meals that really don't do justice to the skills of the chef. Choose à la carte or, better still, from the black-board specials and you'll find the whole experience more rewarding to your taste buds if not your wallet. The menu

The food is consistently wholesome, tasty and unfussily presented

changes regularly to reflect the availability of fresh produce. Everything is rather understated and the selection may appear pedestrian but the mainstream Italian favourites such as pastas (offered either as starter or main) or veal Milanese are done well. The food is consistently wholesome, tasty and unfussily presented. Seafood, fish and game dishes are particularly memorable – look out for scallops of venison served in a perfectly judged berry sauce. Desserts too frequently disappoint. Portions are generally plentiful outwith the cheap deals.

FOOD STYLE **ITALIAN**
LICENSED **YES**
NON-SMOKING TABLES **YES**
WHEELCHAIR ACCESS **No**
OPEN **MON–SAT NOON-2.30PM, 5-11PM**
        SUN 5-10.30PM
PRICE **££**

PIPERS' TRYST

30 McPhater Street   0141 353 5551

Set within the Piping Centre, a wonderfully successful
refurbishment of a striking Victorian church at the top of
Hope Street, this delightfully quaint café bar is actually
part of a small hotel. The location is crucial for it sits at
the edge of Glasgow's theatre land, an area rather poorly
served by decent eating places. The Tryst is small, homely,
comfortable and tranquil apart from 'live Celtic music' at
weekends. The menu is compact so choice is fairly

*The Tryst is
small, homely,
comfortable
and tranquil*

limited (apart from a staggering array
of malts!) but it changes regularly.
As well as unremarkable sandwiches
and snacks, you'll also find excellent
fish (including an ambitious bouill-
abaisse), steak and desserts.

Inevitably, Scottish delicacies such as haggis (including a
veggie version) and black pudding are much in evidence.
While pandering to the city's growing number of tourists
is becoming a tiresome civic obsession, if done as well as
this, all is forgiven. Great value if you take the set lunch
or pre-theatre deal.

FOOD STYLE **SCOTTISH**
LICENSED **YES**
NON-SMOKING TABLES **NO**
WHEELCHAIR ACCESS **YES**
OPEN **MON–THUR 8AM-9.30PM**
      FRI–SUN 8AM-10PM
PRICE **££**

ROGANO

11 Exchange Place   0141 248 4055

The oldest surviving restaurant in Glasgow, Rogano is worth seeing for its remarkable 1930s art deco design alone. Taking its cue from the interior of the Queen Mary, built around the same time, the sheer opulence of the main dining room is unique. Unless on a lavish expense account, you may find the à la carte menu intimidating – you can easily spend £18 on a starter (oysters) and £30 on a main course (lobster thermidor). Value for money? Perhaps not, but the ambience is splendid if you're looking for

The sheer opulence of the main dining room is unique

silver service, crisp white linen table settings and innumerable uniformed staff. Don't panic, there are other options. First, Café Rogano downstairs offers a competitively priced two-course pre/post-theatre meal in marginally less grand but nonetheless impressive surroundings. Or settle down in the relatively informal oyster bar and slurp your way through a plate of oysters, munch a smoked salmon sandwich or tuck into a superior cod and chips. You can sit on the small (usually excessively shaded) terrace in summer if you don't mind passing shoppers peering into your plate.

FOOD STYLE **FISH**
LICENSED **YES**
NON-SMOKING TABLES **YES**
WHEELCHAIR ACCESS **NO**
OPEN **MON–SUN NOON-2.30PM, 6.30-10.30PM; CAFÉ: SUN–THUR NOON-11PM; FRI–SAT NOON-MIDNIGHT**
PRICE **£££**

SANNINO PIZZERIA

61 Bath Street   0141 332 8025

Along with the branch near the King's Theatre in Elmbank Street (0141 332 3565), this perennially popular and much loved basement pizzeria has a character all of its own. The décor is distinctly old-fashioned but in an unstuffy way. The booth style seating can be a little cramped for hefty physiques though there is more space in the central area. The menu is fairly limited by Italian standards. No-one seems to care, for most customers

Most customers come for the pizzas

come for the pizzas. These are churned out endlessly with phenomenal consistency. The bases are thin and yielding, the toppings generous and tasty. The large version is sufficient for two unless one of you is in an especially gluttonous mood. Here's an endearing feature for a kitchen that seems to specialise in mass production – they are perfectly happy for you to invent your own topping. Pastas are equally hard to fault. Desserts are enhanced by fine ice cream. The terrific value lunch (£6.50) and pre-theatre deals are predictably in huge demand.

FOOD STYLE **ITALIAN**
LICENSED **YES**
NON-SMOKING TABLES **NO**
WHEELCHAIR ACCESS **YES**
OPEN **SUN–WED NOON-10.30PM**
        THUR–SAT NOON-MIDNIGHT
PRICE **££**

78 ST VINCENT

78 St Vincent Street   0141 248 7878

Though this looks for all the world like a Parisian brasserie, with its vaulted ceiling, enormous windows, marble staircase and uniformed waiters, the menu tends towards Taste of Scotland rather then French gourmet. The continental touch is unmistakable, however, from the polished if slightly formal service to the impressive wine list. The

The continental touch is unmistakable

seating is cunningly organised in booths framed by coat rails though there are also private rooms available for larger groups. The food is cooked with refinement and presented with great panache. Strong departments are fish, salads and brunch. À la carte prices are steep – sea bream stuffed with wild mushrooms is a wise choice but will set you back around £17 and fillet steak even more. If the set dinner menu causes you to hesitate (three courses for £26.50), opt for the excellent value lunch and pre-theatre offerings but be alert to sneaky supplements. Don't miss out on dessert – who can resist Arran ice cream with strawberries or Belgian chocolate terrine?

FOOD STYLE **SCOTTISH**
LICENSED **YES**
NON-SMOKING TABLES **YES**
WHEELCHAIR ACCESS **YES**
OPEN **MON–THUR 8.30-11AM, NOON-3PM, 5-10PM**
      FRI 8.30-11AM, NOON-3PM, 5-10.30PM
      SAT 9.30-11AM, NOON-3PM, 5-10.30PM
      SUN NOON-3PM, 5-10PM
PRICE **£££**

La TASCA
39 Renfield Street   0141 204 5188

Tapas bars are everywhere in the city these days but few are as popular as this, especially with office parties. Although it's part of a chain, each branch has its own special identity. A hive of frantic and noisy activity at peak times, the multi-level room is crammed full of colourful Spanish memorabilia that deserve some attention in their own right. The menu is strictly tapas (34 of them, each about £3-4) and paella (after 6pm). Vegetarian and gluten free dishes are marked. As well as sangria and beers (including a highly acceptable draught San Miguel), there is an extensive selection of good quality wines (once you get past the house red). Many of the staff are Spanish (and will sing Happy Birthday in their language to prove it) and are hence quite knowledgeable about the food – they'll sort out your piquillo from your pinchito in a jiffy. They do a fantastically skilled and muscular job carrying up to fifteen servings at a time on large round trays.

A hive of frantic and noisy activity at peak times

FOOD STYLE **SPANISH**
LICENSED **YES**
NON-SMOKING TABLES **NO**
WHEELCHAIR ACCESS **YES**
OPEN **SUN–THUR NOON-11PM**
       FRI–SAT NOON-11.30PM
PRICE **££**

TEMPUS

Centre for Contemporary Arts, 350 Sauchiehall Street
0141 332 7959

The CCA is a remarkable building that provides a tranquil haven from the stresses of the city. If you stroll about the displays you'll enter the stylish glass-roofed atrium that houses the café-bar sooner or later. The geometrically precise arrangements of the low wooden tables and cream banquettes are a touch severe perhaps but there's no doubting its strong visual impact

The food is much better than you expect from a café

even if physical comfort is compromised. The designer crockery and cutlery are similarly arresting. The food is much better than you expect from a café, reflecting the commendable ambition of the kitchen. Though you can order simple snacks, there are fresh salad, fish, seafood and game dishes depending on season and availability. Tantalising sauces and spices, many inspired by Far Eastern styles, are deployed with great effect. The menu is likely to evolve over time though it's unclear in which direction. This is an increasingly fashionable spot for corporate functions so you may be unable to turn up on spec.

FOOD STYLE **INTERNATIONAL**
LICENSED **YES**
NON-SMOKING TABLES **YES**
WHEELCHAIR ACCESS **YES**
OPEN **TUE–SAT 11AM-9.30PM**
       SUN 11AM-4PM; CLOSED MON
PRICE **££**

WILLOW TEA ROOMS

217 Sauchiehall Street   0141 332 0521

Glasgow is famous for Art Nouveau and these curious establishments contain some of the finest examples in the city. The Sauchiehall Street branch is probably a more distinguished building – outside and in – than the one at 97 Buchanan Street (0141 204 5242) and has the advantage of a lighter, brighter room with a view on the first floor. Both are largely recreations rather than Miss Cranston's originals but nevertheless will give you a pretty good idea

The real joy though is the elegantly served, expertly brewed tea

of the spectacular design skills of Charles Rennie Mackintosh. The menu is unexciting though there is a fine selection of soups (leek and potato, Scotch broth, lentil). Apart from platters of sandwiches, you are rather restricted to a handful of options (such as haggis and neeps or smoked salmon with scrambled eggs) for main courses. There's a kids menu but frankly youngsters are bound to feel inhibited here. All the food is competently prepared and presented. The real joy though is the elegantly served, expertly brewed tea.

FOOD STYLE **SCOTTISH**
LICENSED **YES**
NON-SMOKING TABLES **YES**
WHEELCHAIR ACCESS **NO**
OPEN **MON–SAT 9AM-4.30PM**
       SUN NOON-3.30PM
PRICE **£**

ZINC BAR AND GRILL
Princes Square   0141 225 5620

Princes Square is an inspired location for this elegant
Conran bar and brasserie. You can sit on the terrace if you
must view the shopping throngs but most will prefer the
impressive inner sanctum. Ignore the pretentious touches
– like the server unfolding your napkin onto your knee (in case you can't do it for yourself), settle back on the big stuffed cushions and get stuck into the marinated olives (£3). The Zinc Dish of the Day (£9 including a glass of wine) may be good value but a choice of one is hardly tempting.

Princes Square is an inspired location for this elegant Conran bar and brasserie

The main courses (including fish, pasta and beef dishes)
range from about £7 to £12 and some of these are highly
accomplished. 'Sandwiches' are not much cheaper
though, to be fair, the portions are sizeable. The food is
generally enjoyable if not outstanding. A small mint with
the coffee wouldn't go amiss. You would hardly guess the
existence of the more upmarket, formal and expensive
Étain restaurant in the adjoining room.

FOOD STYLE **INTERNATIONAL**
LICENSED **YES**
NON-SMOKING TABLES **NO**
WHEELCHAIR ACCESS **YES**
OPEN **SUN–THUR NOON-11PM**
    FRI–SAT NOON-MIDNIGHT
PRICE **££**

MERCHANT CITY AND EAST END

The Merchant City – wedged between the City Centre to its east and the High Street to its west – has become a fashionable residential area in recent years. The historic civic and commercial heart of Glasgow, it boasts many fine buildings and a sense of functional coherence that is almost unique in a modern inner city. At the upper end of the High Street is the majestic Cathedral Precinct that includes the St Mungo Museum of Religious Art (housing Dali's masterpiece depicting the Crucifixion). Also in this area are Strathclyde University and the renascent East End.

ARTA
62 Albion Street   0141 552 2101

Glasgow is famous for ground-breaking interior design and this converted cheese market is well worthy of that description. The ground floor bar is a Hollywood-style extravaganza with huge chandeliers, mock tapestries and vast velvet drapes. The upstairs restaurant, by contrast, has a modernistic décor with bench-like

All great fun but hardly restful

tables, low (backless) stools and tiny flickering candles. The menu is no longer tapas-dominated but retains a Mediterranean flavour. Something has clearly changed in the kitchen for the cooking has improved significantly in the last year or so. Main courses are worryingly hard to see because of the dim lighting but your tongue will attest to their quality. Memorable main dishes include oven baked cod, pizza, and pan fried chicken, the latter served with tagliatelle in a pesto sauce. Lemon tart with ice cream is a pleasant dessert but perhaps try the quirky cheese selection for a change. All great fun but hardly restful – if the shrieking of the revellers at adjoining tables doesn't distract you, the booming music from the bar certainly will.

FOOD STYLE **SPANISH/INTERNATIONAL**
LICENSED **YES**
NON-SMOKING TABLES **NO**
WHEELCHAIR ACCESS **NO**
OPEN **MON–SUN 5-11PM**
PRICE **££**

BABBITY BOWSTER
16-18 Blackfriars Street   0141 552 5055

A unique Glasgow institution, this pub-restaurant (with a few rooms attached) epitomises the Merchant City's rejuvenation – sophisticated, stylish yet utterly unpretentious and firmly rooted in local history. The menu explains the origin of the name (an old Scots dance) and the provenance of the building. In winter, the open fire blazes while in summer you might be tempted into the most attractive little courtyard in the Merchant City. The soups

A unique Glasgow institution

are always interesting. Whether you are a local or a tourist, choose tried and tested Scottish main dishes, including Cullen Skink, haggis (whether authentic or vegetarian), stovies or smoked salmon. Seafood and vegetarian options are consistently good. You may activate the Auld Alliance with confidence (Toulouse sausage, croque monsieur) and that assurance extends well down the wine list. Decent desserts and coffee round off a satisfying experience at a modest price. The occasional live music generates mayhem in this confined space but that is part of its appeal. The upstairs Schottische restaurant is more formal, ambitious and expensive.

Highly recommended

FOOD STYLE **SCOTTISH/INTERNATIONAL**
LICENSED **YES**
NON-SMOKING TABLES **No**
WHEELCHAIR ACCESS **No**
OPEN **MON–SUN NOON-10PM**
PRICE **£(£)**

CAFÉ COSSACHOK
10 King Street   0141 553 0733

Every so often the Glasgow leisure scene throws up a genuinely original creation that transcends established boundaries. Here is a wonderful example. For Café Cossachok is really a kind of mini-arts centre that happens to serve food. There's an art gallery, a programme of folk, jazz and classical music and, of course, the restaurant itself. The dark walls, the sea of shawls on the ceiling, the carved heavy wooden furniture and candlelit

Café Cossachok is really a kind of mini-arts centre that happens to serve food

tables may be suitably traditional but it can all feel a bit oppressive until you've downed a chilled vodka or three. Described as Scotland's first and only authentic Russian restaurant, the cooking meanders into Georgian, Ukrainian, Armenian and other East European genres with great aplomb. The food is wholesome, tasty and thoroughly satisfying though the seasoning may verge on the abrasive here and there. If you're uncertain what to choose, Borscht (beetroot soup) with sour cream is a good bet as are beef stroganoff or Petrushka blintzes. End up with kutuzov (honey and walnut cake).

FOOD STYLE **RUSSIAN/EASTERN EUROPEAN**
LICENSED **YES**
NON-SMOKING TABLES **No**
WHEELCHAIR ACCESS **YES**
OPEN **TUE–SAT 11.30AM -10.30PM**
    SUN 4PM-LATE; CLOSED MON
PRICE **££**

CAFÉ GANDOLFI

64 Albion Street   0141 552 6813

Gandolfi has been around for a quarter of a century yet defies definition being neither a café nor a restaurant but something in between. There's also a new Bar Gandolfi upstairs where snacks are available. Tim Stead's furniture carved from driftwood is justly famous but too many visitors miss John Clark's stained glass windows. Despite the name, the all-day menu is mostly Scottish – or more accurately, Highland. Ingredients are fresh, the cooking confident and unfussy, the presentation straightforward. Favourite dishes include Cullen Skink, Stornoway puddings and smoked venison. Vegetarian options abound. Soups and desserts are almost as good as the main courses. In daylight, at least, lone visitors feel totally at ease. You'll hear occasional mutterings about slowish service but that's perhaps an inevitable price of relentless popularity. When candlelit, at night, the atmosphere is transformed into a bohemian grotto with more romantic connotations. Not especially cheap but you're paying for quality, reliability and popularity.

When candlelit, at night, the atmosphere is transformed into a bohemian grotto

Highly recommended

FOOD STYLE **SCOTTISH**
LICENSED **YES**
NON-SMOKING TABLES **YES**
WHEELCHAIR ACCESS **NO**
OPEN **MON–SAT 9AM-11.30PM**
        SUN NOON-11.30PM
PRICE **££**

CAFÉ MAO
84 Brunswick Street   0141 564 5161

This must be one of the best Oriental fusion restaurants in the city. The décor is ultra-contemporary with large windows, colourful pictures and comfortable seating. The menu is somewhat mystifying at first glance and it's advisable to chat to your server who'll be happy to explain all. The main pitfall is the pungency of the spice, avoidable if you notice the helpful rating symbols. You won't go far wrong if you take spring rolls for a starter followed by Thai or Vietnamese chicken cooked with fresh herbs and served with copious crispy noodles. Alternatively, you might try wok-fried squid or sweet chilli and lemongrass tiger prawns. (You'll gather the chef is a chilli character). Whatever you order, ensure that the Mao beer or at least a jug of Loch Katrine water is on hand to douse the fires. What Chairman Mao would have made of all this is anyone's guess but he would doubtless have approved of the voluble political arguments that the setting seems to inspire.

This must be one of the best Oriental fusion restaurants in the city

FOOD STYLE **CHINESE/VIETNAMESE**
LICENSED **YES**
NON-SMOKING TABLES **YES**
WHEELCHAIR ACCESS **YES**
OPEN **MON–SUN NOON-11PM**
PRICE **££**

CAFÉ OSTRA

15 John Street   0141 552 4433

The Italian Centre springs to life in sunny weather when you can sit out on the terrace. This newish seafood restaurant enhances the continental feel even when you are (as is usual) confined indoors. The dining area is spacious if a little oppressive unless you commandeer the small but much brighter conservatory at the back.

As expected from a sister establishment to Gamba, they are devoted to fishy matters here and that ambition

Ostra's star looks set to rise

mostly pays off. Whether you opt for the modestly priced kipper on toast or throw caution to the wind and select a more expensive daily special, you are unlikely to be disappointed. Fried whitebait with mayonnaise worked a treat with a side salad. Salmon teryaki was a triumph even if the mound of rice, as disarmingly pointed out by the waitress, had collapsed. Desserts don't quite reach the same standard though that may be pot luck. Finish with coffee and tablet. Early days yet but Ostra's star looks set to rise.

FOOD STYLE **FISH**
LICENSED **YES**
NON-SMOKING TABLES **YES**
WHEELCHAIR ACCESS **NO**
OPEN **MON–SAT 10AM-10.30PM**
      SUN 12.30-10PM
PRICE **££(£)**

The CITY MERCHANT
97 Candleriggs   0141 553 1577

Long before the Merchant City became fashionable, the Matteo family pioneered the concept of a top quality fish and seafood restaurant at reasonable prices. Its success was immediate and, with a substantial physical expansion a few years ago, groups and corporate functions muscled in and prices inevitably started to creep up. Nowadays, the set 'daily menu' (around £10 for two courses) is a nostalgic reminder of the early days

The Scottish Seafood Platter is a crustacean spectacular

but if you want an evening meal, be prepared to pay at least double. The array of fish, including species you've never heard of, is startling. The Scottish Seafood Platter (£47.50 for two) is a crustacean spectacular and includes clams, mussels, whelks, prawns, lobster, scallops and oysters. These are all freshly procured and available for your inspection prior to cooking. Keep an eye on the changing blackboard specials and don't be shy about discussing the options with the staff. For carnivores, there's plenty of steak, poultry, beef and game. Desserts look tempting but perhaps sample the unconventional selection of Scottish cheeses.

FOOD STYLE **FISH/SCOTTISH**
LICENSED **YES**
NON-SMOKING TABLES **YES**
WHEELCHAIR ACCESS **YES**
OPEN **MON–SAT NOON-10.30PM**
        CLOSED SUN
PRICE **£££**

CORINTHIAN

191 Ingram Street   0141 552 1101

You must see this one – this building is quite magnificent even by Victorian Glasgow standards. The restaurant has a high vaulted ceiling propped up by massive pillars. The adjoining bar looks odd, the inappropriate furniture totally dwarfed by the sheer scale of the room with its breathtaking glass dome. These cavernous spaces generate a disconcerting acoustic especially when there are few customers. The private dining areas have a much

Full marks to the kitchen for ambition

more intimate feel. The seating, particularly the upholstered benches that line the walls, is exceptionally comfortable and the staff are agree-able even if their lines of communication get crossed occasionally. The menu has a strong Scottish accent with much seafood, fish and game. Full marks to the kitchen for ambition even if the execution is erratic and too often compromised by a tendency to nouvelle cuisine. Soups and desserts generally work best. Prices are high though the set menu offers better value. Black coffee was unpleasantly bitter but the considerate waiter lopped it off the bill.

FOOD STYLE **INTERNATIONAL/SCOTTISH**
LICENSED **YES**
NON-SMOKING TABLES **NO**
WHEELCHAIR ACCESS **NO**
OPEN **MON–THUR 5-10.30PM**
　　　FRI–SAT 5-11PM
PRICE **£££**

The DHABBA
44 Candleriggs   0141 553 1249

Glasgow's growing reputation for fine dining can only be enhanced by imaginative ventures into less familiar culinary territory. If you haven't tried genuine North Indian cooking, you're missing a real surprise. 'The Dhabba concept' is a little hard to grasp – ask the staff who will be delighted to explain. What does become clear is that this is quite unlike the tradi-

Order a Peshwari naan – you won't regret it

tional curry house – everything is lighter, subtler and probably kinder to sensitive digestive tracts. The room is spacious, modern and perhaps lacking in oriental resonance but that's a minor quibble. More problematic is the inconsistency of service, especially on busy evenings, and a reported tendency to serve less than generous portions. The food is, nevertheless, impressive in all departments – especially lamb, seafood and tandoori dishes. If you must have a curry, try this: subzi kofta (dumplings of vegetables and spinach simmered in a spinach based gravy laced with cream) – sensational! Oh, and order a Peshwari naan – you won't regret it. Despite occasional glitches, the Dhabba is a welcome arrival indeed.

FOOD STYLE **INDIAN**
LICENSED **YES**
NON-SMOKING TABLES **YES**
WHEELCHAIR ACCESS **YES**
OPEN **MON–THUR NOON-2PM, 5-11PM**
    FRI NOON-2PM, 5PM-MIDNIGHT
    SAT 1PM-MIDNIGHT
    SUN 1PM-11PM
PRICE **££(£)**

INN ON THE GREEN

25 Greenhead Street   0141 554 0165

Ploughing a lonely furrow for 20 years, this small hotel-restaurant has maintained its standards and popularity despite recent managerial changes. The Green refers to the parkland next to the Clyde that Glaswegians visit in huge numbers to attend rock concerts. Not that you can see it from the slightly oppressive, low-ceilinged cellar restaurant. No matter, there are other distractions such as the original paintings lining the walls and, of course, the piano. Unlike many 'piano bars' in the city, you really will hear quality music, ranging from jazz to folk to classical. The menu revolves around traditional standard Scottish fare – Cullen Skink, haggis and neeps, Arbroath smokies and the like – but you'll also find less familiar tuna, swordfish and partridge creations among the main courses as well as formidable lamb, poultry and steak dishes. The cooking is reliable rather than brilliant. Prices can be high unless you have the set lunch or pre-theatre versions (two courses for £8.50). The East End desperately needs more establishments like this.

The East End desperately needs more establishments like this

FOOD STYLE **SCOTTISH**
LICENSED **YES**
NON-SMOKING TABLES **NO**
WHEELCHAIR ACCESS **NO**
OPEN **MON–FRI NOON-2.30PM, 5-9.30PM**
     SAT–SUN 6-9.30PM
PRICE **££(£)**

The ITALIAN KITCHEN
64 Ingram Street   0141 572 1472

The competition in the pizzeria market is so fierce that one wonders if saturation point has been reached. Apparently not, as the success of this seemingly permanently packed family restaurant testifies. Part of the appeal may be the attractive contemporary décor and furnishings, with gleaming chrome balustrades and bright coloured pictures. The whole edifice seems to glow with irresistible Mediterranean warmth, an effect enhanced by the huge wood-burning oven from within which real flames are clearly visible. The age of the clientele ranges from young to very young, at which the insistent if not altogether unpleasant thrumming of the pop soundtrack is presumably aimed. The tables are mostly well-spaced despite the hubbub and the seating is comfortable. No prizes for guessing the kitchen's key strengths – pastas and the pizzas. The latter are state-of-the-art, thin based, generously topped and thoroughly enjoyable. Seafood fans will appreciate the fish soup. Of the desserts, tarte tatin is the pick of the bunch. Each coffee is adorned, bizarrely, with half a biscuit.

> *The whole edifice seems to glow with irresistible Mediterranean warmth*

FOOD STYLE **ITALIAN**
LICENSED **YES**
NON-SMOKING TABLES **NO**
WHEELCHAIR ACCESS **NO**
OPEN **TUE–THUR AND SUN NOON-10PM**
      FRI–SAT NOON-10.30PM; CLOSED MON
PRICE **££**

OKO

68 Ingram Street   0141 572 1500

First-timers need a short tutorial on how to eat here but the staff reveal the opaque secrets of OKO with patience and good humour. You perch on a stool at a large central table where the dishes sail past on a conveyor belt competing for your attention. The menu is colour coded and takes a bit of studying. Your first decision is whether to choose from the dozens of sushi dishes or to select items from the hot or cold sections. Fish, beef, chicken and vegetables come in various forms (of which teriyaki and tempura are probably the most familiar). You can always opt for a mixture or even just a random sample! Confused? You are not alone. If all else fails, press the call button and someone will rush to the rescue. Prices are fair, considering the quality, but it all adds up quickly. Better value are the twice-weekly buffet nights (on Wednesday and Sunday), you can eat as much as you like in the course of an hour for £15 (£11.50 for students).

First-timers need a short tutorial on how to eat here

FOOD STYLE **JAPANESE**
LICENSED **YES**
NON-SMOKING TABLES **YES**
WHEELCHAIR ACCESS **YES**
OPEN **TUE–THUR NOON-3PM, 6-11PM**
     FRI–SAT NOON-MIDNIGHT
     SUN 5.30-10.30PM CLOSED MON
PRICE **££**

RAB HA'S
83 Hutcheson Street   0141 572 0400

Unbelievably, this compact old building in the heart of the Merchant City contains three facilities in one – hotel, bar and restaurant. Everything is small-scale so if you can get a seat near the open fire on the ground floor, you're doing well. They serve bar snacks here but you should really descend to the cellar for serious eating in a more

A culinary imagination is obviously hard at work

intimate and sophisticated environment. The décor is described as 'contemporary Scottish' – presumably referring to the unobtrusive hints of tartan. Gastronomically we're in Franco-Scottish territory. The soups are rich and tangy, and notable mains include fish, scallops, venison, poultry and haggis, with the odd pasta or salad on offer for vegetarians. A culinary imagination is obviously hard at work – fillet of spiced mackerel or slices of roasted quail breast aren't exactly ten-a-penny even in this chic part of town. Carefully seasoned vegetables are fresh and lightly cooked. The wines are painstakingly selected but pricey (Rioja Gran Reserva around £35). Staff are keen to please and generally succeed.

FOOD STYLE **SCOTTISH**
LICENSED **YES**
NON-SMOKING TABLES **YES**
WHEELCHAIR ACCESS **NO**
OPEN **MON–SUN 5.30-10PM**
PRICE **££**

SMITH'S of Glasgow

109 Candleriggs   0141 552 6539

Perseverance pays! Michael Smith has been plying his trade for years almost unnoticed – perhaps due to his proximity to the City Merchant next door. Thankfully long overdue recognition is arriving. This Parisian style brasserie is all wood panelling and mirrors, informal at lunchtime graduating to white linen in the evenings. The shortish menu is very French with a Scottish accent rather than the other way round. As soon as your order is taken,

The shortish menu is very French with a Scottish accent

along comes a basket of fresh bread, whether or not you've ordered the soup (you should). Chicken liver parfait has an uncannily light consistency. Main courses have some notable fish and vegetarian options, including a perfect omelette aux herbes and a superb risotto. Tender, juicy slices of perfectly cooked braised duck are surrounded by an array of soft pear slices. You may wait a while for your food but relax, it's worth it. Wines are expensive, especially by the glass – you can't have everything. The display cabinet contains the day's desserts – a strawberry tart with vanilla ice cream is beyond criticism. Coffee comes with a tiny biscuit.

Highly recommended

FOOD STYLE **FRENCH**
LICENSED **YES**
NON-SMOKING TABLES **YES**
WHEELCHAIR ACCESS **NO**
OPEN **MON 11AM-5.30PM**
     TUE–SAT 11AM-10PM   CLOSED SUN
PRICE **££**

TRON THEATRE

63 Trongate   0141 552 8587

A major refurbishment of this studio theatre complex some years ago has created welcome new spaces and a subtle change of ambience. The Victorian crush bar that houses the restaurant is not quite as overcrowded as in the early days though at times the sense of eating inside a rugby scrum persists. Of the several ways to eat, the bar menu offers modestly priced snacks that you'll rarely see else-where – Arabian flatbread pizza or salmon fishcake with lime and coriander are two distinguished examples. The pre-theatre (5-7pm Tuesday to Saturday) is more enterprising still with items such as pigeon, steak frites or salmon with courgettes and black olive tampenade. But Sunday brunch is the real treat – how could you resist porridge with raspberry compote, or potato scones with Strathspey mushrooms? For a mere fiver you can have a full Scottish breakfast or its vegetarian equivalent. The whole point of the Tron is to soak up its unique atmosphere. If you enjoy the food, as you probably will, that's a bonus.

The whole point of the Tron is to soak up its unique atmosphere

FOOD STYLE **INTERNATIONAL**
LICENSED **YES**
NON-SMOKING TABLES **YES**
WHEELCHAIR ACCESS **YES**
OPEN **MON–SAT 10AM-8PM**
       SUN NOON-9PM
PRICE **££**

VESPA

17 John Street   **0141 552 4017**

Now part of the Baby Grand group, Vespa is oddly configured, with numerous balconies, recesses and lounges. The kitchen obviously can't compete with Ostra next door but it has some strong points. First, weather permitting, you can sit in either of two outdoor spots – one in the main square, the other within the Italian Centre's elegant courtyard. Second, the choice of wines by the glass is phenomenal – fifty plus is the quoted figure. Starters look

The desserts outshine anything in the vicinity

enticing but do little for real hunger pangs – when the menu says a portion is 'small', you'd better believe it. While main courses (such as pastas, pizzas and salads) are somewhat predictable both in concept and presentation, the blackboard specials (including beef medallions, scallops, monkfish) are much more exciting. They keep the best till last – the desserts outshine anything in the vicinity. Try rich, chocolate torte embellished with fresh berries and vanilla ice cream, or, better still, the biscuits and cheese served on a slab and accompanied by an amusing impression of a swan expertly sculpted from apple slices.

FOOD STYLE **ITALIAN/INTERNATIONAL**
LICENSED **YES**
NON-SMOKING TABLES **YES**
WHEELCHAIR ACCESS **NO**
OPEN **MON–SUN 11AM-11PM**
PRICE **££**

SOUTH SIDE

The South Side is the site of the once notorious
(and now largely redeveloped) Gorbals, the Citizens'
and Tramway Theatres, the Victorian garden suburb of
Pollokshields, the magnificent Burrell Collection, and
Hampden Park with its Scottish Football Museum.
Beyond the lively shopping centre of Shawlands
lies a great swathe of parklands, golf courses and the
extensive residential suburbs of Newlands, Giffnock and
Newton Mearns.

ANDIAMO
223 Fenwick Road, Giffnock   0141 620 3587

Possibly the most improved restaurant on the South Side, Andiamo has overcome initial teething problems and is now packing 'em in most evenings. The décor is ultra-modern with warm colours and heavy yet comfy wrought iron furniture. The interior of the kitchen is clearly visible to diners – always a good sign. The staff are cheery and (mostly) attentive – note ties loosened in precisely the same manner suggesting a casual yet disciplined informality. The menu spans the usual pizzas and pastas (all highly reliable) but there are plenty of meat, fish and salad alternatives. There are some truly bizarre and irritating extra charges – £1 for sharing a pizza, 50p for selecting decaffeinated coffee – whose bright ideas were those? Desserts are excellent as is the coffee, presented with a rock-hard biscuit (for dipping presumably). At midday, soup and sandwiches are available if you aren't ravenous. The early evening menu is superb value if you can slip in before 6.30.

The early evening menu is superb value

FOOD STYLE **ITALIAN**
LICENSED **YES**
NON-SMOKING TABLES **YES**
WHEELCHAIR ACCESS **YES**
OPEN **SUN–THUR 10AM-10.30PM**
     FRI–SAT 10AM-11PM
PRICE **££**

ARIGO

67 Kilmarnock Road   0141 636 6616

Once hailed as the finest Italian restaurant in Glasgow, Arigo's crown has, alas, slipped a little. The spacious multi-level room is as comfortable as ever. And the adjoining wine bar (Arigo Vino) serving breakfast in the mornings and a range of snacks and sputini (Italian tapas) is an enterprising addition. As for the food, you'll still eat pretty well if you choose carefully. Fresh home-baked bread is brought to the table unsolicited. Pasta remains outstanding – large portions, properly seasoned, smothered in delicious herbal sauces. A miserly, crumbling lump of haddock, by contrast, was a mistake, possibly smuggled onto the pre-theatre menu in the futile hope that no-one would notice. Lemon sponge with ice cream and chocolate mousse are both reminiscent of Arigo's good old days.

Pasta remains outstanding – large portions, properly seasoned, smothered in delicious herbal sauces

Service is brisk if impersonal. The house wine remains reliable and good value. The customers are still coming and most seem satisfied so let's hope this old favourite is recovering its form.

FOOD STYLE **ITALIAN**
LICENSED **YES**
NON-SMOKING TABLES **NO**
WHEELCHAIR ACCESS **YES**
OPEN **MON–FRI NOON-2.30PM, 5-10.30PM**
         SAT–SUN NOON-10.30PM
PRICE **££**

ART LOVER'S CAFÉ

House for an Art Lover, Bellahouston Park
0141 353 4779

Well hidden behind the trees of an urban park, the House for an Art Lover is one of those surprising treasures at which Glasgow excels. Charles Rennie Mackintosh designed the house in 1901 but it wasn't built for close to a hundred years. The Café is an extraordinarily elegant space suffused with light even on the gloomiest of days. The walls display changing exhibitions of contemporary Scottish art. The menu is brief but ambitious – just savour

House for an Art Lover is one of those surprising treasures at which Glasgow excels

these titles; tartlet of smoked salmon and asparagus with herbed leaves and mustard seed dressing; purse of artichokes, Israeli couscous with tomato dressing; roast breast of duck, croute of sage and wild garlic with essence of plums. Or just have a bagel from the Café Lites section. There are only nine wines, not a dud among them. Desserts are similarly classy. Finish with a (large or small) cafetiere of coffee or any one of about a dozen teas. Child friendly despite the sophistication.

Highly recommended

FOOD STYLE **INTERNATIONAL**
LICENSED **YES**
NON-SMOKING TABLES **YES**
WHEELCHAIR ACCESS **YES**
OPEN **MON–SUN 10AM-5PM**
PRICE **££**

ASHOKA AT THE MILL

500 Corselet Road, Darnley   **0141 876 0458**

A converted medieval farmhouse in one of the South Side's poorest districts may seem an unlikely setting for an Indian restaurant but the Harlequin Group have pulled it off again. The large building itself is unique, with seating distributed on three floors, plenty of natural light, and a general feeling of spaciousness despite some tables being unaccountably thrust too close together. Families with young children are attracted by the fully equipped indoor play area (£1 entrance) and a large car park. As for the food, undoubtedly the Grand Buffet offers terrific value at £11.95 (cheaper at off-peak times). You start with salads, move on to a finger buffet of pakora-style starters, gorge yourself on the main chicken, lamb or vegetable dishes and conclude (if you are greedy enough) with fresh fruit salad. The major drawback is the limited choice (especially for vegetarians) outwith the buffet – you may need to chat up the genial staff and they'll improvise. Portions are ample even if you eat à la carte.

Families with young children are attracted by the fully equipped indoor play area

FOOD STYLE **INDIAN**
LICENSED **YES**
NON-SMOKING TABLES **YES**
WHEELCHAIR ACCESS **YES**
OPEN **MON–THUR 5-11PM**
       FRI NOON-3PM, 5-11PM
       SAT–SUN 4-11PM
PRICE **££**

BACCO ITALIA
265 Kilmarnock Road   0845 226 7031

Kilmarnock Road aspires to be 'the Byres Road of the South Side' and this unusual wine bar cum bistro is helping it on its way. The name derives from Bacchus, the Roman god of wine and the profusion of Chianti bottles around the room reinforce the point that the grape reigns supreme here. The bright and colourful décor, along with comfortable chairs and informal ambience, raise the spirits as soon as you enter. The staff are good-natured if somewhat inept at times. If you get past the formidable wine list, you may find the menu extremely limited as the traditional Italian favourites are notable by their absence. Most of the dishes are really glorified snacks including soup, fresh salads, smoked salmon or venison, though these are all freshly prepared and extremely enjoyable. Occasional blackboard specialities enable you to venture into the realms of poultry or pasta. Skip the desserts and finish with coffee served with a tiny piece of chocolate. A noble experiment that, with fine-tuning, may just succeed.

The grape reigns supreme here

FOOD STYLE **ITALIAN**
LICENSED **YES**
NON-SMOKING TABLES **NO**
WHEELCHAIR ACCESS **YES**
OPEN **TUE–SAT 9.30AM-10PM**
      SUN–MON: 9.30AM-9.30PM
PRICE **£(£)**

BATTLEFIELD REST
55 Battlefield Rd   0141 636 6955

Once, unbelievably, a tram shelter, this is more than a pretty building though it is worth seeing for that reason alone. The island site is disconcerting at first but you soon forget you're eating in the middle of a busy junction. The Italian owners have established a loyal following. The menu is best described as Italian-Scottish though there's something to suit all tastes. Whether you want a cappuccino and cake in the forenoon or a full evening meal is

Desserts are much more than an afterthought

irrelevant, you will always receive a warm welcome. The lunch and pre-theatre deals are particularly enticing. The onion soup is unrivalled, served with fresh bread. Seafood of all kinds is excellent, as are the more traditional pastas, pizzas and risottos. Desserts are much more than an afterthought and packed with quality ingredients – they will serve you a mouth-watering selection of fresh fruits of the season if you feel guilty about the chocolate cake. Coffee is strong, served with amaretti biscuits. Consistently enjoyable.

Highly recommended

FOOD STYLE **ITALIAN**
LICENSED **YES**
NON-SMOKING TABLES **YES**
WHEELCHAIR ACCESS **YES**
OPEN **MON–SAT 10AM-10PM**
        CLOSED SUN
PRICE **££**

BUONGIORNO
1012 Pollokshaws Road   0141 649 1029

Shawlands is rapidly becoming a centre for outstanding Italian food, a reputation to which this bistro-style restaurant has contributed its share. In its early days, you couldn't swing a spaghetti hoop in here but thankfully the dining area has doubled in size – from minuscule to small. Two long narrow rooms are linked by archways and that helps banish claustrophobia as well as creating a non-smoking space.

But nothing is standard about the cooking

More of a café by day, the candle lit tables in the evenings enhance the atmosphere later. The menu covers the usual soups, pastas and pizzas but nothing is standard about the cooking which is homely and nutritious with some unexpectedly light touches. Fish was once eschewed by the kitchen but that policy has happily changed in response to demand. The house wine is most acceptable, especially as a bottle costs under a tenner. Save room for desserts (provocatively on prominent display) and finish up with good, strong coffee. Service is friendly yet unobtrusive.

FOOD STYLE **ITALIAN**
LICENSED **YES**
NON-SMOKING TABLES **YES**
WHEELCHAIR ACCESS **YES**
OPEN **MON–SAT 9AM-11PM**
     SUN 10AM-10PM
PRICE **££**

CAFÉ SERGHEI
67 Bridge Street   0141 429 1547

The neighbourhood may have seen better days but that hasn't stopped Café Serghei from thriving. Remarkably consistent over many years, this is one of Scotland's best Greek restaurants. First, take a close look at the building – a startling Victorian edifice that was once a bank. The spiral staircase will lead you to a balcony where the views are dizzying even before you knock back a glass of retsina. All the traditional Greek dishes are here but

One of Scotland's best Greek restaurants

especially fine are the starters such as taramasalata or hummus, accompanied by warm, crisp pitta bread, and the classic main dishes (notably kleftiko and moussaka). Vegetarians of various degrees of strictness won't have a problem. Discuss your preferences with the waiters – the kitchen loves to be challenged by unusual requests. Greek dancing and plate-smashing on Friday evenings may not be everyone's glass of Ouzo but the whole thing is carried off with admirable charm and good humour. Prices are modest and the set lunch is truly great value.

FOOD STYLE **GREEK**
LICENSED **LICENSED**
NON-SMOKING TABLES **YES**
WHEELCHAIR ACCESS **YES**
OPEN **MON–SAT NOON-2.30PM, 5-11PM**
       SUN 6-10PM
PRICE **££**

DI MAGGIO'S SOUTH SIDE
1038 Pollokshaws Road, Shawlands 0141 632 4194

A couple of generations of youngsters have benefited from this family-friendly chain. Each branch has its own unique character and this one plays up the sporting theme. The tinted glass frontage protects diners from the curious eyes of passers-by. This has the unintended effect of creating a somewhat gloomy atmosphere that isn't helped by the drab interior décor. The hallmark here is absolute consistency and reliability. Starters range from traditional minestrone to West Coast Mussels to stuffed mushrooms. All are competent if unexciting. The mainstay of the menu is the pizza section. No less than seven are vegetarian and all are expertly executed. Of the pastas, the house speciality Fettuccine Di Maggio (cooked with fresh cream, courgettes, mushrooms and tomato) is delightful. Avoid the house white. The desserts are far better than anticipated – you'll engender much mirth if you order a Dusky Maiden (aka vanilla and chocolate ice cream). The numerous staff are lively and polished.

You'll engender much mirth if you order a Dusky Maiden

FOOD STYLE **ITALIAN**
LICENSED **YES**
NON-SMOKING TABLES **YES**
WHEELCHAIR ACCESS **NO**
OPEN **MON–THUR NOON-2.30PM, 5-11PM**
　　　FRI NOON-2.30PM, 5PM-MIDNIGHT
　　　SAT NOON-MIDNIGHT
　　　SUN 12.30-11PM
PRICE **££**

La FIORENTINA
2 Paisley Road West   0141 420 1585

The designer of this long-established ristorante has recreated an amusingly theatrical southern European setting complete with olive trees. It's somehow appropriate that all this should occupy a Govan building that was inspired, in turn, by a Belgian architectural masterpiece. The spacious dimensions of the dining

Hugely enjoyable and not too pricey

room are matched by an extensive menu, a lengthy wine list and flamboyant service. The cooking is Tuscan in style employing liberal sprinklings of herbs such as rosemary, sage and garlic. Fish, seafood, poultry and veal, grilled or fried in olive oil, are especially successful dishes. Vegetarians are well looked after and rave about the risotto. Desserts often disappoint in Glasgow Italian restaurants but not here – Dolce della Casa comprises layers of Genoese sponge soaked in coffee liqueur, filled and covered with obscenely delicious creams and sauces. Hugely enjoyable and not too pricey unless you venture deep into the à la carte. The main drawback is the uninviting location but you're quite close to the nearby Springfield Quay entertainment complex.

FOOD STYLE **ITALIAN**
LICENSED **YES**
NON-SMOKING TABLES **YES**
WHEELCHAIR ACCESS **YES**
OPEN **MON–SAT NOON-2.15PM, 5.30-10.30PM**
      SUN NOON-2.30PM, 5.30-9.30PM
PRICE **££**

IKAFE
138 Nithsdale Road   0141 423 8128

Though it looks like a café, smells like a café and feels like a café – it isn't necessarily a café. Ikafe is not quite a conventional restaurant either but floats somewhere in the indefinable territory between the two. All of this is academic because the bottom line is that the food is marvellous. The attractive menu is eclectic, the ingredients fresh and the cooking sublime. A thick, luxurious, deeply satisfying soup conjured out of familiar garden vegetables and accompanied by a basket of fresh bread is a light meal in itself. You might jump straight to obscenely tempting desserts and coffee though you'd be missing such treats as grilled halibut with a delicate parsley sauce, Trinidad chicken smothered in an extraordinary melange of apricot, honey and spices, or Caribbean swordfish cooked in a uniquely, well, Caribbean way. Or you can wash down a (not-so-simple) sandwich with a diet coke. Staff are relaxed and attentive despite having to work flat out. Word is spreading and booking is becoming advisable even mid-week.

The bottom line is that the food is marvellous

Highly recommended

FOOD STYLE **INTERNATIONAL**
LICENSED **YES**
NON-SMOKING TABLES **YES**
WHEELCHAIR ACCESS **YES**
OPEN **MON–SAT 9AM-10PM**
       CLOSED SUN
PRICE **££**

KOCHKEMEER

721 Pollokshaws Road   0141 423 9494

Scotland's first Kurdish restaurant is relatively new but already the place is regularly packed out with curious first-timers and returning fans. If they have a free table take it. This is an unmissable experience. The waiters will try to help you understand the menu as the English translations are often impenetrable. Start with

If they have a free table take it

hummus (quite different from the usual Middle Eastern variety) with flatbread, or perhaps soup, a lovely concoction of vegetables, lamb and noodles. Thereafter, you'll probably have lamb or chicken, as there's little else in the meat section, unless you ask for a vegetarian dish based on one of the many sauces. Some examples of main courses: jigeir is barbecued lamb liver with pitta bread, kozisham is spiced lamb, chicken and nuts encased in pastry that goes wonderfully well with kasey (apricot) sauce, goshtibrijour is grilled lamb on pitta with tomato sauce. End with Kurdish tea (if you dare). If you want alcohol, you have to BYO from the off licence across the road. The whole thing comes to about £12 – fantastic value.

Highly recommended

FOOD STYLE **KURDISH**
LICENSED **No**
NON-SMOKING TABLES **YES**
WHEELCHAIR ACCESS **No**
OPEN **SUN–SAT 12.30-10PM**
PRICE **££**

MISE EN PLACE

122 Nithsdale Road   0141 424 4600

After years of neglect, this tranquil corner of Pollokshields is finally coming to life. There's plenty of scope for more but who's complaining when a café as good as this has opened its doors? The business is actually three-in-one – a delicatessen, café and caterer. The ultra-modern premises are delightfully bright, airy and inviting. Sit near the front window for a good view of Britain's most underrated suburb. The staff take a real pride in serving

Even the common-or-garden fruit scone is something of a triumph

even the simplest of items. Order a cup of tea and you get a large pot of your favourite brew served immaculately in matching crockery with a tasty complementary nibble. Even the common-or-garden fruit scone is something of a triumph. If you are peckish, have a more substantial snack but here's a hint – the desserts are very special indeed. No-one will hassle you if you linger, read the paper and let an hour or so slip by. The acme of civilisation, right here in a Glasgow suburb.

Highly recommended

FOOD STYLE **INTERNATIONAL**
LICENSED **YES**
NON-SMOKING TABLES **YES**
WHEELCHAIR ACCESS **YES**
OPEN **MON–FRI 9AM-5PM**
       SAT 9AM-4PM
       CLOSED SUNDAY
PRICE **£(£)**

NEW TURBAN
2 Fenwick Place, Giffnock   0141 638 9635

Once upon a time, the two Giffnock Turbans were con-
nected but apparently this is no longer so. They still share
many features – impressive fish tanks, cubicle seating,
solicitous service. Above all, the standard of cooking is
hard to separate. The New Turban
has opted for a rather more
adventurous and arguably gimmicky menu. If you've always had
a yen for haggis pakora, you'll find
it here and very good it is too.

*If you've always
had a yen for
haggis pakora,
you'll find it here*

Other fusion attempts include an Indian-Mexican dish and
various forms of tikka masala that you won't find easily
on the Subcontinent. Kormas, biryanis and thalis all
deserve a mention but there are few weaknesses. Waiters
don't perhaps have the polish of the Turban, and no
attempt was made to clear away the tablecloth debris of
the admittedly ghastly mess we had made of the main
course. But these are minor cavils. You are sure to enjoy
this as much as the droves of regular customers who
have kept this business going for over twenty years.

FOOD STYLE **INDIAN**
LICENSED **YES**
NON-SMOKING TABLES?
WHEELCHAIR ACCESS **NO**
OPEN **SUN–SAT 5PM-MIDNIGHT**
PRICE **££**

The OSPREY

Stewarton Road, Newton Mearns   0141 616 5071

The Crookfur district of Newton Mearns may have been transformed into a prized commuter area by the nearby M77 but it remains a culinary desert. Thankfully this English style pub is working hard to try to remedy that and has achieved modest success. The spacious car park has stupendous views but is so exposed to the elements that you won't linger there for long. Indeed the blazing log fire in the dining room is something of a necessity most of the year round. Ordering your meal is an amusing ritual of Byzantine complexity involving wooden spoons and table numbers but the good-natured staff will patiently explain what must be done. The menu is an unpretentious affair covering the sorts of dishes you would expect here – vegetable soup, ploughman's salad, cod and chips – though there are a few more audacious items (broccoli and stilton soup, beef and bass ale pie). All good wholesome stuff, loaded with cholesterol and calories, not for the faint hearted in more senses than one.

Ordering your meal is an amusing ritual of Byzantine complexity

FOOD STYLE **BRITISH**
LICENSED **YES**
NON-SMOKING TABLES **YES**
WHEELCHAIR ACCESS **YES**
OPEN **MON–SAT NOON-10PM**
     SUN 12.30PM-10PM
PRICE **£(£)**

PARKLANDS COUNTRY CLUB

Crookfur Park, Ayr Road, Newton Mearns
0141 639 9222

Non-members of this sports and leisure centre are permitted access to the restaurant and its adjoining bar and lounge. These are comfortable spaces where you can have a leisurely beer or coffee while watching the football on a large screen or flicking through the newspapers. The menu of the Brasserie is wide-ranging and hard to classify – Scottish with a light Asian touch perhaps. The cooking is competent with no pretensions to haute cuisine. Starters include chicken noodle soup, steamed mussels, smoked salmon. There are plenty of healthy salads and excellent fish dishes, along with more pedestrian pastas, haggis and poultry. If you prefer to snack, variously filled baked potatoes, sandwiches and (surprisingly good) omelettes are ideal. A steadily improving wine list takes you well beyond the standard Chardonnay. Cappuccino has always been reliable. This is a relaxing, informal and child friendly spot. The young staff are pleasant if often lacking polish. In decent weather you might manage an al fresco lunch.

In decent weather you might manage an al fresco lunch

FOOD STYLE **INTERNATIONAL**
LICENSED **YES**
NON-SMOKING TABLES **YES**
WHEELCHAIR ACCESS **No**
OPEN **SUN–SAT NOON-2PM, 6-9.30PM**
    MON NOON-2PM, 6-8.45PM
PRICE **££**

IL PAVONE SUD
The Avenue, Newton Mearns   0141 616 0011

A suburban shopping precinct is an unpromising site for a decent restaurant but this one has struck lucky with this delightfully informal pizzeria. Located slightly off the main walkway, you may miss it entirely if you're not concentrating. Once through the doors you sense you have entered a restful refuge from the stress of shopping. The room is spacious, bright and colourful, the staff welcoming and the menu appealing. You're not obliged to order a full

A restful refuge from the stress of shopping

meal but you probably will. There's a special emphasis on seafood suggesting that this is the chef's forte and indeed any of the fish dishes – including shellfish – are excellent. The safe Italian standbys – minestrone, pasta, pizza, risotto – are all reliable. The wine list is well constructed but you may find even the house wine a little too pricey if you're drinking by the glass. As expected, coffee is good. Background music is occasionally a mite too intrusive in the reverberant acoustic.

FOOD STYLE **ITALIAN**
LICENSED **YES**
NON-SMOKING TABLES **YES**
WHEELCHAIR ACCESS **YES**
OPEN **MON–SAT 10AM-10PM**
     SUN NOON-10PM
PRICE **££**

PETERS SOUTH SIDE

205 Fenwick Road, Giffnock   0141 621 1903

At the last count there were three branches of Peters yet there is nothing remotely chain-like about this delightful little restaurant. Space is tight but it doesn't seem to matter. Locals return again and again for one reason only – proprietor Peter Pang knows exactly what his customers want. He provides consistently first-rate cooking in pleasant surroundings served by friendly staff at reasonable prices. The menu is so devoid of pretension that it verges on the pedestrian. Don't be fooled. This is traditional Scottish cuisine at its finest. Your evening starts with a miniature complementary appetiser of meat or cheese containing splendidly elusive flavours – a portent of greater things to come. Favoured starters include changing soups, char-grilled crab cakes and asparagus salad. For a main course, take fish – halibut, trout and sea bass are all exquisitely prepared and presented with al dente vegetables. A smooth, creamy yet not too sweet cheese cake is the star dessert turn. The pre-theatre (around £11 for two course) is astonishing value but you'll have to book.

Traditional Scottish cuisine at its finest

Highly recommended

FOOD STYLE **SCOTTISH**
LICENSED **YES**
NON-SMOKING TABLES **YES**
WHEELCHAIR ACCESS **YES**
OPEN **MON–SUN NOON-2PM, 5-9PM**
PRICE **££(£)**

RISTORANTE PREGO

108 Ayr Road, Newton Mearns   0141 639 8496

Of all the eateries in this multicultural strip, Prego is arguably the best. An ingenious deployment of colours and mirrors makes the most of a confined space. The pictures on the walls are worth a second look and may occasionally be for sale. The menu is smallish, particularly the set lunch and pre-theatre deals, and vegetarians may have to switch to the à la carte. Freshly baked bread is proffered generously as you ponder the

What a pleasure to get a decent portion of fish

options. As well as the obligatory minestrone, the chef can turn his hand successfully to other soups. Pastas are superb, lightly seasoned and imbued with clever combinations of herbal flavours. Seafood is handled confidently – and what a pleasure to get a decent portion of fish even from the pre-theatre! Vegetable accompaniments receive equally assured treatment. The house wine is acceptable (and available as a half-carafe) though some of the Sicilian bottles may interest you more. Desserts are hit and miss – jump straight to the rich coffee, served with almond biscuits and mints.

FOOD STYLE **ITALIAN**
LICENSED **YES**
NON-SMOKING TABLES **NO**
WHEELCHAIR ACCESS **YES**
OPEN **MON–SAT 5.15-9.30PM**
        CLOSED SUN
PRICE **££**

ROMA MIA
162 Darnley Street   0141 423 6694

East Pollokshields is perhaps an unlikely location for
Mediterranean food but the gamble seems to have
worked. Even when the nearby Tramway theatre is out of
action, Roma Mia buzzes with discerning regulars, many
of Italian origin. Massimo and
Giusseppe have extended and
refurbished the dining area in
tasteful pinks and blues. The
effect is bright, spacious and
welcoming. As soon as you

The chef will concoct virtually anything for you if he has the ingredients

enter, you feel positive vibes. The menu has many of the
usual pasta dishes, along with plenty of fish, chicken,
seafood, meat (especially steak) and vegetarian choices,
though there are no pizzas. The attitude of the kitchen is
relaxed – the chef will concoct virtually anything for you if
he has the ingredients. The cooking is refined and deeply
impressive. Wines are well chosen but many will be content with the house red – a beauty. À la carte prices are
far from cheap but they come generously garnished. If
you are able to take advantage of the pre-theatre meal,
your options are restricted but the value is unbeatable.

Highly recommended

FOOD STYLE **ITALIAN**
LICENSED **YES**
NON-SMOKING TABLES **NO**
WHEELCHAIR ACCESS **YES**
OPEN **MON–SAT NOON-2.30PM, 5.30-10.30PM
SUN 6.30-10.30PM**
PRICE **££(£)**

TURBAN TANDOORI
2 Station Road, Giffnock   0141 638 0069

This longstanding and locally revered restaurant is probably the finest curry house in the city and perhaps one of the top three in the UK. Consistently in the premier league for at least the last decade, the Turban shows no sign of losing its magic touch. The surroundings are pleasurable (even if you don't care to be met at the door by a goldfish tank), the lighting subdued, the music unobtrusive. (Try to ignore the persistently ringing phone). Cubicalised seating confers a sense of privacy. The service is professional and friendly. As for the food, where to begin? My suggestion is pakora (aubergine, cauliflower or plain vegetable), followed by the inspired pistachio korma or the astonishing Turban Special tandoori 'sizzla'. Apparently, ostrich, crocodile and kangaroo meat is offered for the delectation of more adventurous souls. Whatever you choose, you can't go far wrong. For extras, select a bowl of saffron rice and a sweet paratha and you are all set for one of life's unrivalled pleasures. They don't come much better than this.

The Turban shows no sign of losing its magic touch

Highly recommended

FOOD STYLE **INDIAN**
LICENSED **YES**
NON-SMOKING TABLES **NO**
WHEELCHAIR ACCESS **YES**
OPEN **SUN–SAT 5PM-MIDNIGHT**
PRICE **££**

MY TOP TEN
WEST END

STRAVAIGIN 2

8 Ruthven Lane   0141 334 7165

The menu is truly extraordinary, spanning continents. If Louisiana crab cakes or mussels with coriander don't appeal, what about free range duck egg on chapati?

NO. 16

16 Byres Road   0141 339 2544

You sense that everyone concerned is striving for excellence and it shows. No. 16 edges ever closer to the number one slot in the West End.

CITY CENTRE

THE BUTTERY

652 Argyle Street   0141 221 8188

This much loved Glasgow institution traces its pedigree back to 1869 and is well worth its numerous awards ever since. Very special, very enjoyable and very expensive (except for the set lunch).

MINSKYS

Hilton Hotel, 1 William St   0141 204 5555

A mock New York style deli, the terrific self-service buffet is actually about as British as you can get. If you have room, the desserts are outstanding.

MERCHANT CITY

SMITHS

109 Candleriggs   0141 552 6539

Long overdue recognition for this Parisian style brasserie is arriving at last – perseverance pays! You too may wait a while, but relax, when the food arrives it's worth it.

BABBITY BOWSTER

16-18 Blackfriars Street   0141 552 5055

A unique Glasgow institution, this pub-restaurant epitomises the Merchant City's rejuvenation. Sophisticated, stylish yet utterly unpretentious.

SOUTH SIDE

PETERS SOUTH SIDE

205 Fenwick Road, Giffnock   0141 621 1903

Space is tight in this delightful little restaurant but it doesn't seem to matter. Savour consistently first-rate cooking served in pleasant surroundings by friendly staff at reasonable prices.

IKAFE

138 Nithsdale Road   0141 423 8128

Ikafe is neither a café nor a conventional restaurant either but floats somewhere between the two. All of this is academic because the bottom line is that the food is marvellous.

ROMA MIA

162 Darnley Street   0141 423 6694

As soon as you enter, you feel positive vibes from this Mediterranean haven in East Pollokshields. The chef will concoct virtually anything for you if he has the ingredients.

TURBAN TANDOORI

2 Station Road, Giffnock   0141 638 0069

Probably the finest curry house in the city, the Turban shows no sign of losing its magic touch. Whatever you choose, you can't go far wrong.

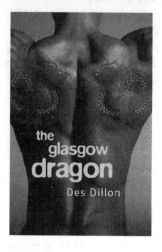

The Glasgow Dragon
Des Dillon
ISBN 1 84282 056 7 PB £9.99

What do I want? Let me see now. I want to destroy you spiritually, emotionally and mentally before I destroy you physically.

When Christie Devlin goes into business with a triad to take control of the Glasgow drug market little does he know that his downfall and the destruction of his family is being plotted. As Devlin struggles with his own demons the real fight is just beginning.

There are some things you should never forgive yourself for.

Will he unlock the memories of the past in time to understand what is happening?

Will he be able to save his daughter from the danger he has put her in?

Nothing is as simple as good and evil. Des Dillon is a master storyteller and this is a world he knows well.

The authenticity, brutality, humour and most of all the humanity of the characters and the reality of the world they inhabit in Des Dillon's stories are never in question.
LESLEY BENZIE

It has been known for years that Des Dillon writes some of Scotland's most vibrant prose.
ALAN BISSETT

Des Dillon's exuberant mastery of language energises everything he writes.
JANET PAISLEY

FICTION

The Road Dance
John MacKay
ISBN 1 84282 040 0 PB £6.99

Milk Treading
Nick Smith
ISBN 1 84282 037 0 PB £6.99

The Strange Case of RL Stevenson
Richard Woodhead
ISBN 0 946487 86 3 HB £16.99

But n Ben A-Go-Go
Matthew Fitt
ISBN 0 946487 82 0 HB £10.99
ISBN 1 84282 014 1 PB £6.99

Grave Robbers
Robin Mitchell
ISBN 0 946487 72 3 PB £7.99

The Bannockburn Years
William Scott
ISBN 0 946487 34 0 PB £7.95

The Great Melnikov
Hugh MacLachlan
ISBN 0 946487 42 1 PB £7.95

The Fundamentals of New Caledonia
David Nicol
ISBN 0 946487 93 6 HB £16.99

Heartland
John MacKay
ISBN 1 84282 059 1 PB £9.99

Driftnet
Lin Anderson
ISBN 1 84282 034 6 PB £9.99

Torch
Lin Anderson
ISBN 1 84282 042 7 PB £9.99

The Blue Moon Book
Anne MacLeod
ISBN 1 84282 061 3 PB £9.99

The Glasgow Dragon
Des Dillon
ISBN 1 84282 056 7 PB £9.99

Six Black Candles [B format edition]
Des Dillon
ISBN 1 84282 053 2 PB £6.99

Me and Ma Gal [B format edition]
Des Dillon
ISBN 1 84282 054 0 PB £5.99

The Golden Menagerie
Allan Cameron
ISBN 1 84282 057 5 PB £9.99

FOOD & DRINK

The Whisky Muse: Scotch whisky in poem & song
various, compiled and edited by Robin Laing
ISBN 1 84282 041 9 PB £7.99

First Foods Fast: how to prepare good simple meals for your baby
Lara Boyd
ISBN 1 84282 002 8 PB £4.99

Edinburgh and Leith Pub Guide
Stuart McHardy
ISBN 0 946487 80 4 PB £4.95

POETRY

Drink the Green Fairy
Brian Whittingham
ISBN 1 84282 045 1 PB £8.99

The Ruba'iyat of Omar Khayyam, in Scots
Rab Wilson
ISBN 1 84282 046 X PB £8.99 (book)
ISBN 1 84282 070 2 £9.99 (audio CD)

Talking with Tongues
Brian Finch
ISBN 1 84282 006 0 PB £8.99

Kate o Shanter's Tale and other poems
Matthew Fitt
ISBN 1 84282 028 1 PB £6.99 (book)
ISBN 1 84282 043 5 £9.99 (audio CD)

Bad Ass Raindrop
Kokumo Rocks
ISBN 1 84282 018 4 PB £6.99

Madame Fi Fi's Farewell and other poems
Gerry Cambridge
ISBN 1 84282 005 2 PB £8.99

Scots Poems to be Read Aloud
Introduced by Stuart McHardy
ISBN 0 946487 81 2 PB £5.00

Picking Brambles and other poems
Des Dillon
ISBN 1 84282 021 4 PB £6.99

Sex, Death & Football
Alistair Findlay
ISBN 1 84282 022 2 PB £6.99

Tartan & Turban
Bashabi Fraser
ISBN 1 84282 044 3 PB £8.99

Immortal Memories: A Compilation of Toasts to the Memory of Burns as delivered at Burns Suppers, 1801-2001
John Cairney
ISBN 1 84282 009 5 HB £20.00

Poems to be Read Aloud
Introduced by Tom Atkinson
ISBN 0 946487 00 6 PB £5.00

Men and Beasts: wild men and tame animals
Valerie Gillies and Rebecca Marr
ISBN 0 946487 92 8 PB £15.00

Caledonian Cramboclink: the Poetry of
William Neill
ISBN 0 946487 53 7 PB £8.99

The Luath Burns Companion
John Cairney
ISBN 1 84282 000 1 PB £10.00

Into the Blue Wavelengths
Roderick Watson
ISBN 1 84282 075 3 PB £8.99

Sun Behind the Castle
Angus Calder
ISBN 1 84282 078 8 PB £8.99

Burning Whins
Liz Niven
ISBN 1 84282 074 5 PB £8.99

A Long Stride Shortens the Road
Donald Smith
ISBN 1 84282 073 7 PB £8.99

THE QUEST FOR

The Quest for the Celtic Key
Karen Ralls-MacLeod and
Ian Robertson
ISBN 0 946487 73 1 HB £18.99
ISBN 1 84282 031 1 PB £8.99

The Quest for Arthur
Stuart McHardy
ISBN 1 84282 012 5 HB £16.99

The Quest for the Nine Maidens
Stuart McHardy
ISBN 0 946487 66 9 HB £16.99

The Quest for Charles Rennie Mackintosh
John Cairney
ISBN 1 84282 058 3 HB £16.99

The Quest for Robert Louis Stevenson
John Cairney
ISBN 0 946487 87 1 HB £16.99

The Quest for the Original Horse Whisperers
Russell Lyon
ISBN 1 84282 020 6 HB £16.99

ON THE TRAIL OF

On the Trail of the Pilgrim Fathers
J. Keith Cheetham
ISBN 0 946487 83 9 PB £7.99

On the Trail of Mary Queen of Scots
J. Keith Cheetham
ISBN 0 946487 50 2 PB £7.99

On the Trail of John Wesley
J. Keith Cheetham
ISBN 1 84282 023 0 PB £7.99

On the Trail of William Wallace
David R. Ross
ISBN 0 946487 47 2 PB £7.99

On the Trail of Robert the Bruce
David R. Ross
ISBN 0 946487 52 9 PB £7.99

On the Trail of Robert Service
GW Lockhart
ISBN 0 946487 24 3 PB £7.99

On the Trail of John Muir
Cherry Good
ISBN 0 946487 62 6 PB £7.99

On the Trail of Robert Burns
John Cairney
ISBN 0 946487 51 0 PB £7.99

On the Trail of Bonnie Prince Charlie
David R Ross
ISBN 0 946487 68 5 PB £7.99

On the Trail of Queen Victoria in the Highlands
Ian R Mitchell
ISBN 0 946487 79 0 PB £7.99

BIOGRAPHY

The Last Lighthouse
Sharma Krauskopf
ISBN 0 946487 96 0 PB £7.99

Tobermory Teuchter
Peter Macnab
ISBN 0 946487 41 3 PB £7.99

Bare Feet & Tackety Boots
Archie Cameron
ISBN 0 946487 17 0 PB £7.95

Come Dungeons Dark
John Taylor Caldwell
ISBN 0 946487 19 7 PB £6.95

Luath Press Limited
committed to publishing well written books worth reading

LUATH PRESS takes its name from Robert Burns, whose little collie Luath (*Gael.*, swift or nimble) tripped up Jean Armour at a wedding and gave him the chance to speak to the woman who was to be his wife and the abiding love of his life. Burns called one of *The Twa Dogs* Luath after Cuchullin's hunting dog in *Ossian's Fingal*. Luath Press was established in 1981 in the heart of Burns country, and is now based a few steps up the road from Burns' first lodgings on Edinburgh's Royal Mile.

Luath offers you distinctive writing with a hint of unexpected pleasures.

Most bookshops in the UK, the US, Canada, Australia, New Zealand and parts of Europe either carry our books in stock or can order them for you. To order direct from us, please send a £sterling cheque, postal order, international money order or your credit card details (number, address of cardholder and expiry date) to us at the address below. Please add post and packing as follows: UK – £1.00 per delivery address; overseas surface mail – £2.50 per delivery address; overseas airmail – £3.50 for the first book to each delivery address, plus £1.00 for each additional book by airmail to the same address. If your order is a gift, we will happily enclose your card or message at no extra charge.

Luath Press Limited
543/2 Castlehill
The Royal Mile
Edinburgh EH1 2ND
Scotland
Telephone: 0131 225 4326 (24 hours)
Fax: 0131 225 4324
email: gavin.macdougall@luath.co.uk
Website: www.luath.co.uk

INDEX